POLICY STUDIES IN EMPLOYMENT AND WELFARE NUMBER 17

General Editors: Sar. A. Levitan and Garth L. Mangum

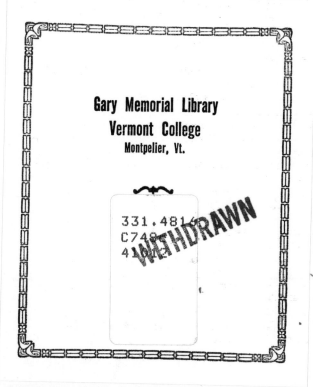

Corporate Lib: Women's Challenge to Management

Edited by

**Eli Ginzberg and
Alice M. Yohalem**

The Johns Hopkins University Press, Baltimore and London

The Johns Hopkins University Press, Baltimore, Maryland 21218
The Johns Hopkins University Press Ltd., London

Library of Congress Catalog Card Number 72–12371
ISBN 0–8018–1475–8 (cloth)
ISBN 0–8018–1474–X (paper)

Library of Congress Cataloging in Publication data will be found on the
last printed page of this book.

To
Four Friends of My Youth

Who taught me that woman, though a gender,
Should be treated as an individual ——
A lesson that most men have yet to learn.

Contents

List of Tables

List of Figures

Foreword

The Executive Programs of the Graduate School of Business, Columbia University, under the leadership of Associate Dean Hoke Simpson, sponsored a Conference on Women's Challenge to Management at Arden House in the fall of 1971, attended by representatives of business, government, and universities. The conference was organized in the belief that the 1970s would see radical changes in the role of women in American management and that it was both the obligation and an opportunity for a graduate business school to assist in exploring relevant issues and to help in pointing the directions for action.

This volume contains the principal papers prepared for and the key presentations delivered at the conference, together with introductory and concluding chapters that frame the problem in broader perspective. This book is responsive to the promptings of the conferees that these materials be made more widely available to those in managerial positions in business, education, and government who must find answers to the challenges presented by women seeking entrance into professional and executive employment.

Eli Ginzberg

Graduate School of Business
Columbia University

Contributors

Charles De Carlo
President, Sarah Lawrence College

Mary Sarah Fasenmyer
Dean, School of Education, Catholic University of America

Eli Ginzberg
A. Barton Hepburn Professor of Economics, Graduate School of Business, and Director, Conservation of Human Resources, Columbia University

William Goode
Professor of Sociology, Columbia University

Elizabeth Janeway
Author

Juanita Kreps
James B. Duke Professor of Economics, Duke University

James W. Kuhn
Professor of Industrial Relations, Graduate School of Business, Columbia University

Michael H. Moskow
Assistant Secretary of Labor, U.S. Department of Labor

Valerie K. Oppenheimer
Research Sociologist, University of California, Los Angeles

Rosemary Park
Professor of Education, University of California, Los Angeles

Edward A. Robie
Senior Vice President, Equitable Life Assurance Society

Phyllis Wallace
Vice President for Research, Metropolitan Applied Research Center

Alice M. Yohalem
Research Associate, Conservation of Human Resources, Columbia University

Corporate Lib: Women's Challenge to Management

1

The New Reality

Eli Ginzberg and *Alice M. Yohalem*

In assessing social change, it is always difficult to distinguish between minor variations and basic transformations. History never moves at a measured pace. Even the unusual and the spectacular can come and pass without leaving permanent changes in their wake. Yet if one were forced to wager, it is a good bet that the fall and winter of 1971–72 represents a watershed in the womanpower revolution which has been gathering momentum since World War II.

In this six month period one can point to the following developments. First was the revision of Order Number 4 of the U.S. Department of Labor, previously limited to minorities, which extended the coverage of the mandate for affirmative action by government contractors in providing equal employment opportunities to include women. By a single stroke, federal contractors, the employers of one-third of the nation's workers, were required to develop procedures for the nondiscriminatory utilization of the female labor force.

As an outgrowth of this development, the Department of Health, Education and Welfare, which has the primary responsibility for dealing with universities holding federal contracts,

1

withheld approval of a number of affirmative action plans submitted by leading universities on the ground that they did not sufficiently satisfy the criteria for setting goals and specifying policies and procedures that would encourage the appointment of a larger number of qualified women to nontenured and tenured positions.

Next, after a great many abortive efforts, a coalition of women activists finally prevailed upon Congress to pass an equal rights amendment to the Constitution. Informed observers believe that ratification by the states will not be long delayed.

Also, Congress expanded the reach of the Equal Employment Opportunity Commission (EEOC) to include local and state government employees—an important arena of female employment. At the same time, enforcement initiatives available to the EEOC were increased by enabling the commission to bring class actions before the federal courts.

In addition to these significant developments on the governmental front, the fall and winter of 1971–72 saw a mounting concern on the part of large employers to acquaint themselves with the new reality. Having been under increasing pressure, from governmental agencies as well as from voluntary groups, since the passage of the Civil Rights Act of 1964, to increase their efforts to expand employment opportunities for blacks and other minorities, the corporate world read the revision of Order Number 4 as the signal that it was intended to be. They were put on notice by the federal government that they had to develop affirmative action plans aimed at overcoming deficiencies in the utilization of women throughout their organizations. A conspicuous deficiency characteristic of most employing organizations was the disproportionately small number of women in management, particularly in higher management.

A large number of nonprofit organizations, including major universities, foundations, political parties, religious agencies and hospitals, also moved to get in step with the times by appointing one or more women to positions of power and prestige.

If additional proof were needed that women in management had become an "in" subject, all doubts dissolved in face of the large number of conferences, seminars, and training sessions that were organized by consulting organizations to cater to the burgeoning demand for orientation and assistance in responding to the new pressures. While this record of events is no guarantee that the revolution in womanpower has entered a new phase, the evidence does point in that direction.

The present effort was planned just before the breakthrough occurred. It is directed toward probing the subject of women in management by exploring its historical antecedents; by assessing the barriers and potentialities for constructive action; and by weighing the broader social implications of any significant changes in women's role in the work world. Its objective is understanding. If the many complex dimensions of the theme are delineated and appraised, there is good prospect for constructive action. In the absence of understanding, there is likely to be much activity, but little action; much turmoil, but little change.

A brief view of the current status of female workers will serve as background to the contributions that follow. At the present time, there are about 31½ million women in the labor force representing over 40 percent of all workers in the United States. Most of these women are highly concentrated within a few so-called female occupations. About 15 percent of all male workers but less than five percent of all females were salaried managers or officials in 1971. While women comprise two-fifths of the total labor force, they account for only 15 percent of total managerial employment, seven percent of all physicians and 21 percent of all professionals outside the fields of education and health. Thus, the representation of women at the top levels of the job ladder is disproportionately small in relation both to the size of the female labor force and to total employment in these occupations.

The first paper is a response to women's challenge by a representative of progressive management who admits past injustices and seeks to make amends. Edward A. Robie expects improved female job opportunities to occur because women will become an increasingly larger component of the labor force; their demands will receive wider support from male allies; and management cannot any longer afford to waste so valuable a pool of talent. He refutes the notions that serve to perpetuate sex typing of occupations and contends that if top executives commit themselves to support non-discriminatory treatment of women, lower levels in the organization will take heed and respond accordingly. Robie concludes by making specific recommendations for improving the recruitment, assignment, and work schedules of female managers.

Valerie Oppenheimer challenges this optimistic view of a self-initiating and self-implementing reform by management. She emphasizes that demographic changes in female labor force participation, rather than a reversal in employer attitudes, will be the catalyst for the expansion and improvement of women's job opportunities. Dr. Oppenheimer notes that work is assuming increasing importance in the lives of women as they recognize the advantages of a continuing relationship to the labor market. Accordingly, women's aspirations will rise and they will no longer be satisfied with the kinds of jobs that they were willing to tolerate when they had peripheral relations to work. Growing reliance on two earners per family and a rising number of divorcées will further intensify pressures for an expansion of female job opportunities. Moreover, female aspirations will be raised as more women attain high educational levels. College educated women will press to enter male dominated occupations, the more so because such traditional female fields as teaching are failing to expand.

The barriers that face women in a college community are delineated by Rosemary Park, who pays special attention to the difficulties they encounter in obtaining good positions in university administration and teaching. Since the educational preparation of females does not differ significantly from that of males, at least to the baccalaureate, Dr. Park concludes that the underrepresentation of American women at the higher occupational levels reflects a combination of male discrimination in association with low female aspirations, which, in turn, are the outgrowth of societal biases.

Unlike corporate management, the university power structure is more diffuse. Department heads, overwhelmingly male, tend to be highly resistant to change, and without their toleration, if not active support, it is very difficult to institute significant changes in personnel policy. However, the practice of rotating department chairmen will eventually lead to the selection of younger men, who are likely to be more sympathetic to women's demands. Dr. Park contends that the university community can no longer treat sex discrimination on the campus as a "non-problem."

Mary Sarah Fasenmyer emphasizes the role of the educational system as a reinforcer of social values, including those that restrict women's aspirations and goals. She believes that the guidance of females has been particularly remiss in failing to provide them with counterweights to negative family influences that discriminate against girls. The pervasiveness of sex discrimination is underscored, in her view, by the preference shown males even in female fields, such as teaching, where males preempt most administrative positions and, in the present unbalanced labor market, are given preference in hiring and promotion.

Professor James Kuhn, drawing on his professional expertise with respect to labor markets and on his own family history rooted in the rural Northwest, reminds us that in earlier times the farm wife was a full partner in the family's economic enterprise. The full-time homemaker without economic significance is a phenomenon of an industrial urbanized society. However, Professor Kuhn suggests that there is a large reserve of female workers which is much greater than our employment data suggest. He makes a strong plea for more jobs to meet the legitimate need of these potential workers and points out that the total number of jobs must be sufficient to employ not only women but also blacks and other minorities who seek similar opportunities.

Phyllis Wallace's paper synthesizes the principal research investigations dealing with the underrepresentation of women in preferred employment and discusses the many obstacles that have barred them from equal consideration for leadership positions. She echoes the recurring theme that societal expectations of women's *proper* role have served to limit female representation at high occupational levels and to create distinctive male and female labor markets with pay and promotional structures much more favorable to men. At the managerial level, income differentials between the sexes may be even larger than generally acknowledged because valuable fringe benefits and other perquisites are often restricted to males. Dr. Wallace concludes her analysis by presenting some similarities and differences in the antidiscrimination approach to women and to racial and other minorities.

Juanita Kreps places the evidence about sex inequalities into perspective by proceeding beyond data that demonstrate constraints on women's upward mobility to produce explanations and rationales for their poor showing. She suggests that certain assumptions that have been used to rationalize denial of access to higher rank are losing their validity—such as claims of excessive turnover—although she cautions that others, such as geographical immobility, will remain as long as husbands' careers and children's needs take precedence over mothers' work. Dr. Kreps calls for a reconsideration of career priorities and family responsibilities to permit greater flexibility in life styles for both sexes, a plea that is repeated by others in this volume.

William Goode examines the implications of broadened work opportunities upon the personal lives, particularly the marital arrangements, of women managers, while expressing grave doubts about the speed with which such new opportunities will become available. Dr. Goode focuses upon the budgeting of time and energy as central to the question of women's ability to handle responsibilities at home and at work, for if no changes are to be made in the family system, women managers may have no option but to remain childless. However, he sees continuing modifications in the life patterns of the most successful women that will allow them more of the freedom of choice now permitted to successful men.

While Elizabeth Janeway agrees that men will not easily be persuaded to yield high places to women, she believes that the growing activity of women in their own behalf will be a major force in achieving this goal. She deplores the lack of social support for alternative suppliers of child care and sees such support at lower occupational levels as essential for women who seek to qualify for top jobs because it will permit them to maintain con- tinuity of employment while they move up the ladder. Janeway challenges the observation that it is the lack of a wife that ham- pers female achievement. She asserts that ambitious, qualified women lack access to *staff*, since this is the real function a wife performs for her successful husband.

While it is generally recognized that pressure by women them- selves will help to force change, the action of government may prove crucial. Thus, Michael H. Moskow's description of the Affirmative Action program whereby federal contractors must formulate plans for the more effective utilization of women and minorities at all occupational levels is of special interest. Since these contractors include most of the country's largest employ- ing institutions, and since failure to comply with the new regula- tions can lead to severe financial loss, this program is likely to have a wide ranging impact upon the nation's employment policies.

A provocative note is struck by Charles De Carlo, who presents a challenge to women to consider whether their attempts to gain access to management are worth the effort. He suggests that women may make more of a contribution by creating new social institutions than by trying to invade an increasingly obso- lescent work structure. However, he recognizes that neither women nor minorities are sufficiently powerful to institute basic changes, and so, for the time being, they will have to concen- trate on influencing management to accommodate their needs by revising their employment policies.

The concluding chapter attempts to sort out the wide variety of viewpoints adumbrated by the several writers, each of whom, understandably, has drawn heavily on specialized knowledge and experience. Yet despite many differences, it is the consensus that rampant discrimination exists; that it is deeply embedded; and that it will not yield easily. Nevertheless, all agree that the future will see a lowering of the barriers against women in man- agement. The rate of progress will depend on many unknowns,

7

including the policy of the federal government; the drive and competence of women's organizations; the rate of economic growth; and the degree of interaction between the youth and black revolutions and the women's revolution. But women have challenged management and a reasonable prognosis is that management, women, and the nation will never again be the same.

2
Challenge to Management

Edward A. Robie

If Alexis de Tocqueville were visiting the United States today, he would be likely to describe our corporate order as a "maleocracy," and no one would argue with the accuracy of his observation. A twentieth century de Tocqueville would also go on to note, with little fear of contradiction, that the attitudes on which this maleocracy is based are changing, especially among a high proportion of the most influential men and women in this country. Our observer would not, I am afraid, see much evidence of *action* change. He would no doubt conclude, correctly in my judgment, that the walls of the corporate maleocracy were pretty thick and the weapons of those assaulting those walls were still not very powerful, in spite of growing dedication to tearing the walls down.

Let me make my point of view clear at the outset. Business and industry should give a high priority to revising the channels of access to management so that a greater percentage of qualified women can reach management positions. There are a lot of good reasons why we should do this, and no good reasons why we should not.

In purely quantitative terms, it is estimated that between 1970 and 1980 the female labor force will increase by about six million persons.[1] This quantitative growth is bound to have qualitative impact: no work organization can effectively digest such a large change in the composition of its labor force without making changes in the composition of its managerial ranks.

Beyond the question of quantitative change lies the realm of *attitude* change. In the past women's feelings about their role in society generally, and their treatment with regard to employment specifically, were neither strong nor vocal. There was no organized movement of any consequence among women with the specified goal of changing women's role in society. Cynthia Epstein has perceptively noted in speaking of this that "women's place in society and in the home may have limited their horizons but it has not generated fears for the stability of society."[2] A woman's revolution has never been a real threat, in other words. This state of affairs is certainly changing. Women as a group are becoming increasingly frustrated and increasingly more vocal about this frustration. A new "revolution of rising expectations" has begun.

As educational opportunities have substantially improved, new goals have been established, and the possibility of real progress toward these goals has appeared. Such a situation typically engenders a sense of deep dedication in those involved. They can be expected to fight with a religious fervor to achieve their newly defined goals. I believe a strong below-the-surface feeling of frustration exists among many of our most intelligent and, by the standards of today's system, successful career women, most of whom are not a part of any organized movement. If, as they seek a greater degree of equality, these ostensibly quite peaceful women do not meet appropriate responses, more and more of them may seek to change the system in highly unconventional and abrasive ways. We have witnessed this scenario with minority groups within the United States, with peoples in the later

---

[1] U.S. Department of Labor, Bureau of Labor Statistics, "The U.S. Economy in 1980," *Monthly Labor Review*, vol. 93, no. 4 (April 1970): 25.

[2] Cynthia Fuchs Epstein, *Woman's Place: Options and Limits in Professional Careers* (Berkeley: University of California Press, 1970), p. 1.

stages of colonial rule, and during the more conventional types of political revolution.

Women are not alone in their desire to change current attitudes about their status. The chances for change are reinforced by evidence that a large percentage of men are also sympathetic to women's goals. A Louis Harris poll, for instance, found that by a plurality of 44 percent to 39 percent a representative sample of men supported efforts to strengthen or change women's status in society while only 40 percent of women favored these efforts, with 42 percent opposed to them. As a matter of fact, the phrase "women's lib" elicited more positive than negative responses from men, while the reverse was true for women.[3]

The female responses to this survey are more revealing when one breaks down the answers by types of respondents and finds a great disparity in how different categories of women replied. The strongest support for efforts to improve women's status came from divorced or separated women (61 percent versus 36 percent for widowed and 38 percent for married); strong support also came from black women (60 percent, versus 37 percent for white women), and women with postgraduate education (58 percent, versus 38 percent for high school graduates). Significantly, women under 30 were stronger supporters (46 percent) than women 50 and over (35 percent). These data suggest that we can expect growing support for efforts to improve women's status.

From a management point of view, perhaps the strongest argument for revision of employment practices so as to increase the number of women in management positions is that industry can simply no longer afford to waste so valuable a resource. As society expands and becomes more complex, so do the problems of the organizations serving it. Every available source of talent must be tapped if we are to cope effectively and competitively with these problems. It is entirely possible—I would even say probable—that women represent a source of superior talent to

[3] Louis Harris and Associates, *The Virginia Slims American Women's Opinion Poll* (New York, 1971), p. 4.

the company that can successfully recruit them and provide them with the experience necessary to qualify for management jobs.

Other arguments can be advanced to support the creation of opportunities for women in management, including the simple fact that our country is founded on the principle of equality of opportunity, and we talk a lot about that to ourselves and to the rest of the world.

I need not dwell any longer on the arguments for inclusion of women in management but it is important to make clear that the viewpoint of this paper is a personal one, not intended to represent a general management position. I am a businessman and have spent most of my career in jobs related to personnel administration. While I feel concern for the human and ethical dimensions of the problem of equality of women, and am interested in and, I hope, not without some understanding of the sociology of the problem, my approach is essentially a pragmatic one. As I view the situation, both business and women would gain by more effective utilization of women in management. Thus for me the central question is *how* to bring about this change, how, in brief, to channel more qualified and motivated women into our managerial structure.

Superficial changes within the existing system of management recruitment and patterns of promotion are essential, but, as I will argue, they cannot suffice. What is needed is more management questioning of traditional attitudes and encouragement of new and fundamentally different approaches based on a continuing willingness to confront the facts. In this paper I will briefly review the current situation, pinpoint certain problems, and indicate the approaches that seem to me to hold the most promise for rational, nondiscriminatory solutions.

We are all well aware that most jobs are typically held almost exclusively either by men or by women. Thus there are distinct "male" and "female" job markets. Victor Fuchs points out in his major study of the wage differential between men and women that "one of the most striking findings is how few occupations employ large numbers of both sexes. Most men work in occupa-

Figure 1. CONCENTRATION OF MALE AND FEMALE
EMPLOYMENT, 1969

PERCENT OF TOTAL EMPLOYMENT, BY SEX

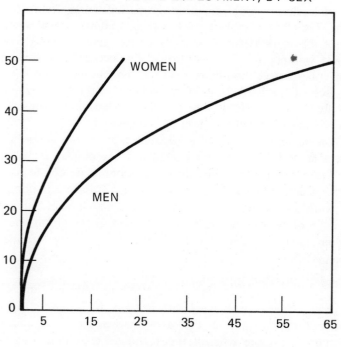

NUMBERS OF OCCUPATIONS

Source: Janice Neiper Hedges, "Women at Work: Women Workers and Manpower Demands in the 1970's," *Monthly Labor Review*, vol. 93, no. 6 (June
1970): 20.

tions that employ very few women, and a significant fraction of women work in occupations that employ very few men."[4]

If there remains any question on this point, Valerie Oppenheimer's recent study conclusively demonstrates that a distinct female job market does exist. Her study of census data from 1900 through 1960 demonstrates that the distribution of women in the work force has remained highly disproportionate for the entire period, even though the percentage of the labor force that is female almost doubled during the period, rising from 18% to 33%. The data in table 1 present these findings. At present, the female job market is an extremely narrow one. A quarter of all women workers are clustered around five occupations—secretary, retail salesperson, household worker, bookkeeper, and elementary school teacher.[5] Half of all women workers are employed in only 21 occupations, whereas half of all male workers are more broadly distributed in over 65 occupations.

Women, then, do indeed predominate in certain areas of employment and are virtually excluded from others. Included in this latter group are management positions and jobs leading to management. When I refer to management I am not limiting myself to those responsible for directing the activities of substantial numbers of people, but rather to a much larger group who are responsible for significant decisionmaking in an organization. In business, beginning "male" jobs are frequently preparatory to entry into management; typical "female" jobs on the other hand are not. A woman is simply expected to improve and refine whatever skills are associated with her job. If she meets expected standards and remains in the labor market she is advanced. A secretary is a more efficient typist and a better office organizer than a stenographer. Her functions, however, do not significantly change. She is just attached to a higher level boss.

While a man, to one degree or another, has access to the

---

[4] Victor R. Fuchs, "Differences in Hourly Earnings Between Men and Women," *Monthly Labor Review*, vol. 94, no. 5 (May 1971): 14.

[5] U.S. Department of Labor, Women's Bureau, *1969 Handbook on Women Workers* (Washington, D.C., 1969), p. 96.

Table 1. Women in Disproportionately Female Occupations,[a] 1900–1960

| Year[b] | Females as a Percent of Total Labor Force | Percent of Female Labor Force | | Ratio of Observed to Expected |
		Expected in these occupations[c]	Observed in these occupations	
1900	18	21	74	3.5
1910	20	30	83	2.7
1920	20	33	86	2.6
1930	22	35	89	2.5
1940	24	36	89	2.5
1950	28	40	86	2.2
1950*	28	37	85	2.3
1960	33	38	81	2.1

SOURCE: Valerie Kincade Oppenheimer, *The Female Labor Force in the United States: Demographic and Economic Factors Governing its Growth and Changing Composition* (Berkeley: University of California Press, 1970), p. 69.

[a] An occupation is considered "disproportionately female" when women form a higher proportion of the workers in the occupation than they do in the labor force as a whole.

[b] The 1960 occupational classification system is not quite comparable to the 1950 system. Data adjusted to the 1950 census are available for 1900 through 1940, but data comparable to 1960 are available only for 1950. For this reason, 1950 data are presented twice: "1950" is according to the 1950 system, and "1950*" is according to the 1960 occupational classification system.

[c] This is the percentage of the female labor force that would have been observed in these occupations if their sex compositions had been the same as the sex composition for the work force as a whole.

decisionmaking process where leadership is exerted, action initiated, and the product determined, the woman "oils the works"— helps matters to run more smoothly and efficiently. The parameters of female jobs are vastly more confining than those of male jobs, and up to now this state of affairs has been commonly accepted without serious question by both management and employees alike. Even where women occupy higher level jobs which meet my broad definition of "management," women tend to have helper oriented titles, such as executive assistant or assistant manager.

Role differentiation based on sex in the labor market is, of course, reflective of patterns found in society as a whole and in its institutions. Despite the traditional notions about women which perpetuate these patterns, the basic assumption of this analysis is that we have no rational basis for assuming that sex, per se, is a significant factor in terms of ability to assume and perform managerial jobs. Our major objective, then, is to expand managerial job opportunities and to counteract discriminatory attitudes that not only limit access but also make it difficult for a woman to achieve a top management position even if she does enter the management world. Any management aiming at this objective must first raise and try to cope with questions about the reasons for the attitudes that perpetuate what is, in effect, a bifurcated labor market.

What is most interesting is not so much the characteristics attributed to women, as the assumptions that these characteristics are not appropriate for managerial jobs *and* that they are universally applicable to the female population. For example, gentleness as against strength; emotionalism as against rationalism; submissiveness as against leadership. Yet in recent years management literature has been full of reports on research which might be interpreted to indicate that a more "female" approach to management might produce rather better results than the traditional "male" approach. In terms that the late Douglas McGregor made famous, is a woman more inclined to be an autocratic Theory "X" leader, or a more participative Theory "Y" leader?

But it doesn't make much sense to carry this argument very far because the definition and the universality of the so–called female characteristics are so questionable and controversial in the first place. Whether or not the characteristics common to most women are different from those common to most men, it is evident from everyday observation and experience that many women are aggressively strong, rational, natural leaders and many men are the opposite. If there is an "average" behavior for each sex, there is lots of deviation from it.

Incidentally, I might observe that the same characteristics are often defined quite differently when displayed by a man and when displayed by a woman. For example, one of the most frequently cited qualities of women is their alleged ability to influence men subtly. A particularly perceptive woman manager suggested to me that this ability in male business executives is usually called "leadership."

With reference to female and male leadership characteristics, I have often observed that girls in coeducational environments exhibit greater leadership strengths in their early school activities than do boys. Apparently, adult attitudes begin to catch up with them as they grow older when girls start adapting to their expected supporting role.

Perhaps the most persistent argument rationalizing failure to recruit and train women for management positions is that they are more turnover prone than men. This naturally makes good sense to most male managers who recall losing many young women employees to marriage, or because of the mobility of a husband. How much this "good sense" is based on hard fact may be quite another question, since with a little prodding these same managers might be reminded that their record of keeping young men isn't very good either. In my experience, if you can keep half of your high potential male college input for the first five years, you are doing pretty well.

One of the strongest influences operating to maintain the present structure of the job market is to be found in the attitudes women have about themselves. The Louis Harris poll referred to earlier, revealed a deep-seated lack of confidence among females in the managerial ability of their own sex; for example, working women prefer a male boss to a female boss 8 to 1.[6] No doubt this lack of self-confidence leads to doubts about their ability to handle supervisory responsibility and to lower expectations in terms of advancment.

Also reinforcing and maintaining the bifurcated structure of the job market are the attitudes women have about crossing into the "male" labor market. Out of attitudes about women's general role are born strong incentives to remain within the "female"

[6] Harris, *Women's Opinion Poll*, p. 24.

market. For many women, no doubt the incongruity between the "female" role as our society defines it and a potential "masculine" executive role brings various personality conflicts into play. They may refrain from seeking or accepting prospective "nonfeminine" jobs because they fear being unhappy or unsuccessful in their "feminine" role. One resolution of this conflict is, of course, identification with the dominant group on the part of nonmembers. Some women managers, for example, end up "out-maleing" the males!

The positive incentives to remain in the accepted role for their sex are not limited, of course, to women. Really, the incentives for men to remain in the male labor market, and the disincentives for them to enter the female market, are even more pronounced. Generally, a man found in the female labor market finds his very masculinity suspect by both sexes, or it's taken for granted that he has little ambition. When we recently suggested to the female supervisor of an all female key-tape unit the possible desirability of recruiting some males, she remarked that "only gay men would be interested."

As the structure of the job market influences, reinforces, and perhaps sustains attitudes, so too are these attitudes projected onto the structure. For example, a kind of "attitude spillover" occurs in the sense that the very placement of a woman in a given position eventually tends to define that position as being one of servicing or helping with limited room for advancement.

It is not necessarily true that the traditional women's jobs in business are not objectively a good training ground for management. But as long as they are *perceived* as "helping" roles, the jump from such a position into management remains exceedingly difficult. The example comes to mind of the capable secretary to a manager who by virtue of her proximity to her boss learns a great deal about what he does and how he does it. Although in an extraordinarily good training position in many important ways, the secretary (if female) is not expected to assume the role her boss fills at any future date. She is expected, rather, to be his assistant or, if very competent, an assistant to a higher level manager. Her status and her rewards in her role as helper are often not directly related to her functions, but rather to the status of the person she works for. "Achievement" for females is simply not associated with leadership. Hence, the female helper's perspective on management tasks, and most important, her boss's estimate and *her* expectation of her ability to assume the management role, remain untouched by her proximity to management. It is surprising, but paradoxically true, that someone who learns all about the management role is not being groomed for management.

At the same time one realizes that even if the secretary were to bolt the system and become a manager, the environment would not be conducive to her successful fulfillment of this role. Neither the woman in question nor her subordinates would be geared to expect responsible leadership. If subordinates are reluctant to follow a woman manager because she happens to be a woman, she is less likely to succeed as a supervisor. The old "helper" expectation tends to create a self-fulfilling prophecy.

It occurs to me that a somewhat similar set of circumstances in a small business context frequently produces an opposite result. Consider a female who assists her husband in the operation of his business. When her husband dies suddenly, it is not thought strange for the widow to take over the leadership role in the business. Perhaps a study has been done on this—it would be most interesting to learn what has happened in a number of situations where women assume management positions with many less societal constraints than we seem to find within large businesses.

Any business manager who believes, as I do, that the status of women should be improved, has a responsibility to seek, to suggest, and to encourage change. I shall try to shoulder that responsibility but I do so with the belief that changes will not occur easily, nor that the status of women in business will improve rapidly. Yet I am convinced that changes are occurring at an accelerating rate and that this acceleration will continue, bringing about a slow but sure movement toward greater equality of the sexes in management ranks.

The single most encouraging factor I see is the greater influence of youth in the decade ahead. Peter Drucker, in a recent provocative article entitled "The Surprising Seventies," points out that the center of population gravity in this country moved from the 35 to 40 age group in 1960 all the way down to 17-year-olds in 1964. The 17-year-old group increased in size every year until 1971, and remained the largest single age group for this entire six-year span. By 1975, the dominant age year will have risen, but only to 21 or 22.[7] All the studies I have seen show young people to be more egalitarian about sex than their elders. I was impressed the other day by what a middle-aged female manager had to say about *her* attitude toward young people. "I feel much more comfortable talking to our young, high potential managers than to our older managers," she told me. "They seem to accept me much more as a person, rather than as a female who used to be a secretary. I have to watch what I say to the older men, and to watch how they react to what I say. I always have to be on my guard with them."

In any particular company, effective change is most likely to happen if senior management takes a clear-cut position, communicates it to lower levels, and acts as though it means what it says. The precise words are not important, but they must clearly say that the company wants to improve the utilization of the human resources available to it, and that this specifically includes more attention to women. Senior executives have numerous opportunities to reiterate such a policy statement once made and if they really want action they will ask for progress reports to monitor what happens. This ensures that the subject will automatically come up for helpful review, discussion, and reemphasis.

Of course the senior executives themselves make specific decisions affecting the status of women that will be carefully watched by their subordinates. For instance, are women considered as candidates for the board of directors, and are qualified women

---

[7] Peter F. Drucker, "The Surprising Seventies," *Harper's Magazine,* July 1971, p. 36.

appointed? Are women considered as candidates for promotions to the officer level, and how many female officers are there? Are women appointed to important company committees? Are women invited to attend high level meetings? Are these meetings held at clubs where women are not admitted? It is a significant fact that membership in the prestigious Economic Club of New York is not open to women and I presume this may be the case in a number of other private groups of high level business executives, formed not for social but for business purposes. Do specifications to executive search firms make clear that qualified women candidates are desired?

In recent years a great deal of attention has been focused on legal measures to improve the status of minorities. Now that legislation covers discrimination against women because of sex, I guess we will have to change our terminology, since women are in the majority. How important an influence are the equal opportunity laws which, of course, now exist on local, state, and federal levels? Based on my experience with legislative attempts to improve the status of blacks and Puerto Ricans, I think government pressure can be very helpful, although I must admit that it can also be aggravating, and that it sometimes seems to me to be overdone or misguided. However, the attitude of the company toward government compliance efforts is the really critical factor.

If the government compliance effort is viewed primarily as a threat, then each meeting with government officials is likely to be like another round in a boxing match between adversaries, with the company dodging around trying to avoid a knockdown blow. If, on the other hand, such meetings are viewed as a dialogue, albeit sometimes quite spirited, in a joint effort to determine how and when to achieve improvement in employee status, then constructive ideas and approaches can and do result.

Some government compliance people may make a boxing match inevitable, and some company people may do the same—in this case, it only takes one side to make a fight—but in our experience, most compliance people have been cooperative and have respected our point of view and our efforts, as we have theirs, even though we have had lots of disagreements. It remains to be seen just how vigorously legislation on equal opportunity for women will be enforced. The government itself does not appear to have a very good record in providing equal opportunity for women.

I mentioned that government pressure can sometimes be misguided. I consider current attempts to interpret the law to equate maternity with sickness as poor public policy. Without taking the time to discuss all the pros and cons, there would be a strong incentive for employers to avoid hiring career-oriented women until after childbearing years if they are forced to pay sick pay for what is, after all, a discretionary disability. Maternity leave is quite another question, and more liberal leave arrangements are, in my judgment, overdue.

One of the most frequent reasons given as to why there are not more women in management positions is that there aren't many who are qualified. Pressed for detailed specifications to document the required qualifications, most managers would probably specify education and experience.

Let us take a look first at education. Few managers would agree on the kind of education that is the best preparation for a management career, unless a highly specialized career in a professional area were specified. Based on recruiting activity, however, it is clear that the graduate business schools provide an educational background eagerly sought and dearly paid for by most leading companies. Just within the last decade these schools have begun to admit women. In 1971 Harvard Business School graduated 29 women in a class of 754, and the University of Chicago 7 in a class of 280. I think it is safe to say that ten years ago the number of female graduates from both schools was close to zero.

The University of Chicago Business School is stepping up recruitment of women because it is expected that companies will be more aggressively seeking out female graduates in the next few years. On the matter of equality of salary offers made to male and female graduates at Chicago, the story was told by Lawrence Jones, assistant dean of students of the graduate school of the University of Chicago, that one company that offered a girl a subpar salary found itself boycotted by prospective applicants of *both* sexes on that campus. All the girl did was to post the letter containing her offer on the bulletin board!

Placement officers at several leading female undergraduate colleges where we inquired note an increase in recruiting interest by companies seeking women but no significant increase in interest in business careers on the part of their students. There is still a tendency, they say, for women to take courses to help them qualify for teaching, even with the oversupply of teachers. We might reasonably expect, however, that as teaching jobs remain relatively hard to find, an increasing supply of well-educated women will be available to those businesses who seek them out and provide them with opportunity.

Of course, recent college graduates are not the only good recruitment sources for potential managers. Most companies keep a weather eye out for the young man with limited education who starts at the bottom and whose head so consistently sticks up above his peers to warrant a series of promotions. Nearly always such a young man will, with adequate guidance and encouragement, pick up some advanced education at night under a tuition refund program. The same weather eye ought to be focused on promising women, including of course, those who come equipped with college degrees but who are placed in low level positions and are overlooked as a source of management talent. It is an interesting and profitable exercise for a company to identify the top 10% of its females according to performance, and then to identify the top 25% of that group according to potential. At one firm, a number of the best female clerical workers have obtained college degrees under a tuition refund program. Those who show this kind of ability and motivation can be excellent candidates for promotion to management jobs for which only males are considered normally.

As a final suggestion on recruiting, I wonder if the special management development programs designed for high potential new B.A.'s and M.B.A.'s could be opened to high potential older female B.A.'s and M.A.'s wishing to return to the labor market. Personally I doubt if refresher academic training would always be needed, but if it were, such courses could be taken prior to return either under a special program designed by a university for this purpose, or simply by judicious choice of appropriate courses after consultation with a prospective employer.

Where there is a shortage of competent people, such as experienced systems analysts, programmer analysts, and supervisors of teams composed of these people, an innovative company might consider developing its own refresher course designed for women with programmer experience who should be returning to the labor market in increasing numbers in future years. Entry qualifications could be set at a high level, and only superior performers need be maintained in the program. Pay could be modest during training, since a marketable skill would be taught without any guarantee either of employment or willingness to accept a job, but the returns to companies could be handsome in terms of making available topnotch candidates for hard-to-fill jobs.

So far I have dealt with educational qualifications—let me turn now to experience. I might start by referring again to the data processing systems field, because even where women appear to have the educational background for the work, there still remains the question of the *experience* that may be needed to qualify for management jobs.

The data processing systems field has frequently been mentioned as a new, high demand–low supply area where sex-typing has not occurred. The thought has been expressed that women should have—and perhaps have had—an unusually good opportunity to qualify for management jobs in this field. I do not see much evidence that this is the case, either among manufacturers of equipment or among users.

The technical data processing career route has not turned out so far to be the most fruitful source of talent, male or female, for the management jobs responsible for designing and administering data processing systems. Thus, even though at the programmer level there is a substantial supply of competent women, this has not yet proven to be an access point of substantial importance to management jobs. In insurance companies these jobs have tended to go to specialists, such as actuaries. Equipment manufacturers tend to have emphasized the sales side of their business as the major access to management, and, as a result, there are very few women managers in these companies who have risen from programming positions.

Because this is still a relatively new and growing field in which women have shown considerable interest, and in which many of them have demonstrated unquestioned technical competence, it seems to me a matter worth further exploration. What career patterns have developed in different companies and industries? What variations are there in the use of women? What factors are responsible for these variations? What are the likely future trends?

These questions remind me of a comment made to me during a recent discussion with a group of female managers. "Nobody knows how well we can do in management jobs because no company gives enough of us a chance to get the experience that would prove or disprove the allegations that we won't do well." It seemed to me when I heard that comment that my paper might be most accurate and most effective if I only quoted that simple statement.

Cynthia Epstein's excellent book, *Woman's Place*, contains some perceptive advice for women seeking careers in management and for the company seeking such women.[8] After a careful geodetic survey of the reefs of discrimination in the professions, Dr. Epstein charts a course designed to keep to the channels and to avoid the reefs. I liked particularly her suggestion that women should "not permit their own self-consciousness to cause them to overreact. Women who are professional but not especially forward or aggressive, who try to be gracious as women and not deny their sex, are said to be able to make the best impression on men and gain acceptance."[9]

Perhaps a word is in order here about the broad definition of management that I have used, that is, those holding jobs respon-

---

[8] See Epstein, *Woman's Place*, chap. 5, pp. 167–97.
[9] Ibid., p. 195.

sible for significant decisionmaking rather than jobs responsible for directing the activities of substantial numbers of people. In most large business firms, a high proportion of the key jobs are held by professional people, such as lawyers, actuaries, and systems specialists, and many of these people spend a significant proportion of their time *both* practicing their profession *and* directing the work of others. As Dr. Epstein has pointed out, these are among the most appropriate kinds of jobs in which women can get a foothold in the management hierarchy.

In addition to finding better avenues for introducing more women into the ranks of management, any management really anxious to make use of womanpower has to start thinking about the degree to which its conventional system of compensation and traditional working conditions might be modified to be more attractive to qualified women. Quite a bit has already been written about this and I am not sure I have many new ideas so I will not dwell on the subject at length, but will try to quickly review some of the kinds of things that need to be considered. Incidentally, most of the changes in compensation schemes and in working conditions will serve to attract women to business not just in management jobs but in all capacities.

First of all, working schedules need to be made more flexible. Business is already experimenting quite successfully with the four-day week, which seems particularly well adapted to women who want their weekends off and also want one day a week for the myriad personal and household chores that go with managing a family.

Part-time work needs more testing. We recently were faced with the possibility of losing one of our most valued and competent women, a top systems expert. She felt that she had to devote more time to her family than was possible while holding down an extremely demanding full-time job with us. We worked out a part-time arrangement whereby we get her services on a rather flexible basis for about three days a week and, although we would prefer to have her full-time, we are delighted to have her for three days rather than not at all. In another case, we just rehired a young mother who had started with us right out of high school, gotten her college degree at night through our tuition refund program with a brilliant academic record, then left to have a child. She is working on a schedule that varies both with her needs and our work pressures, averaging three days a week. She is handling a demanding analysis and report writing assignment with great distinction.

Some companies have worked out successful arrangements for women to arrive about ten o'clock and depart around three, or for variable starting and quitting times with a center core of standard hours, such that a full day is worked each day. By and large, these arrangements are not appropriate for supervisory jobs, but there may be possibilities worth exploring here for other types of management jobs.

Communication facilities are rapidly reaching the point where people in certain demanding specialized jobs will be able to communicate to work rather than commute to work. I am not an expert on sophisticated communications networks and how computer terminals can be arranged to facilitate programming and systems work being done at remote locations. However, I understand from the experts that this is technically quite possible now, and it may well be that before too long a qualified housewife could spend part of her day as a manager in a large bureaucracy, while working in her own home. An incidental benefit from this might be that it would cut down on meetings!

Provisions for taking care of children have been much discussed, and it appears that government arrangements may be increasingly available for child care during working hours. This certainly could enable more mothers to stay in the labor market if they so wished, including mothers who have achieved managerial status. Presumably a break of several months for pregnancy would be much less of a barrier than a break of several years.

In addition to flexible work scheduling, attention needs to be given to more flexible compensation arrangements. Greater employee option in compensation arrangements is a desirable employee relations objective for both women and men. While I earlier mentioned some doubt about the desirability of equating

27

maternity leave with sick leave, it certainly is conceivable that in a compensation program that provides options, the opportunity might be made available to a woman to pick a benefits program that offered pay for maternity leave or even child care instead of some other part of the benefits package, such as group life insurance or pension benefits, that seems less suited to her particular needs. Providing this kind of option is a tricky business and work has only just begun on how to deal with the complicated questions of the relative costs; definition of the kinds of options that would be attractive to employees; antiselection problems, etc., but it is a promising development for employee relations generally and for bringing more women into management in particular.

As I conclude this discussion I am impressed and humbled by the complexity of the problem. More research to yield more knowledge is certainly needed, yet research must be thorough and it must be interpreted with great care. If research showed women managers to be more effective than men, it might be because we insisted on greater qualifications for a prospective woman manager than for a man. We have some data on black and white life insurance agents that raise this kind of difficult interpretative question. If women are less successful, it might be because of the inimical social context, the self-fulfilling prophecy we discussed earlier.

Our dilemma is increased by the fact that the existence of a rational exclusively female job market, based on the availability of relatively high quality women at a relatively low price for jobs like secretary, clerk, nurse and teacher, tends to perpetuate the attitudes and values that support an irrational exclusively male job market. One wishes that a frontal attack on this bifurcated structure could be made, putting men in "female jobs" as well as women in "male jobs." But, as Valerie Oppenheimer points out in her study of "The Female Labor Force in the United States":

Once recourse has been made to female labor to provide quality labor at a low price, employers tend to get used to relatively well-educated workers (standards have been going up, not down) who have been working for much less than men who have received a comparable education. To substitute men to any considerable extent would require either a rise in the price paid for labor or a decline in the quality of the labor, or both. Unless there are some very compelling reasons for it, it seems unlikely that many female occupations of this type will radically change their sex composition.[10]

So we are left with the necessity for the practical but piecemeal approach.

In any event, we must not be discouraged by the depth of the traditions undergirding our "maleocracy" and the size of the challenge facing us. As Daniel Bell has commented:

Time, said St. Augustine, is a threefold present: the present as we experience it, the past as a present memory, and the future as a present expectation. By that criterion, the world of the year 2000 has already arrived; for the decisions we make now, in the way we design our environment and thus sketch the lines of constraints, the future is committed. . . . The future is not an overarching leap; it begins in the present.[11]

By taking measures today which anticipate the challenges arising out of women's demands and the obvious need for more talented management, we can avoid problems that will foreseeably arise tomorrow.

[10] Oppenheimer, *The Female Labor Force*, p. 102.
[11] Daniel Bell, ed., "Toward the Year 2000: Work in Progress," *Daedalus*, Summer 1967, p. 639.

3
A Sociologist's Skepticism

Valerie K. Oppenheimer

It certainly is reassuring to know that Edward Robie's heart and, hopefully, the hearts of many other senior management people are in the right place. Presumably, we can therefore expect a rapid integration of females into management within the next few years.

However, I find it interesting that so much of his paper is devoted to discussing what management *should* do, rather than what is actually being done—by business firms in general or by his own firm in particular. Being of a skeptical frame of mind, by nature as well as training, I question whether much, in fact, *is* being done. In truth, I wonder whether his presentation is but another example of the first half of that famous slogan—"Promise her anything, but give her. . . ." Let us hope it is more than the secretary's proverbial bottle of Arpege at Christmas time.

Perhaps I am being unjust. If so, and great breakthroughs are being attempted, I do wish Robie had tried to share some of these successes with us and, particularly, the concrete problems involved in trying to achieve them. For problems certainly abound and unless they are perceived and solved, women will form no larger a proportion of executives ten years from now than they do today in spite of the best intentions on the part of everybody concerned.

I want to focus my discussion upon the reasons for continuing pressures for women to get into management, as well as into other higher level jobs such as the male professions and, in fact, into all male occupations.

In the first section of his paper, Mr. Robie outlines what he feels are some of the good reasons why more women should be drawn into management. I found them most unconvincing. If I were in personnel management, it would take many more persuasive reasons than these to get me moving. For example, Mr. Robie argues that by 1980 six million more women will be in the work force and "no work organization can effectively digest such a large change in the composition of its labor force without making changes in the composition of its managerial ranks."[1] I should like to point out that 31 million women are already in the labor force without any accompanying breakthroughs into management. I don't see how an additional six million would necessarily lead to a radical departure in employer policies.

Furthermore, I see no particular reason why the size of the female labor force, or more pertinently, the sex composition of the workers in a firm, will affect the ratio of males to females in management. Many large scale white collar firms traditionally have had very high proportions of female workers—banks, insurance companies, the telephone company, etc. Yet, there is no comparable representation of women in management. Thus, if most female employees are in the usual dead end female jobs, I fail to see what difference it makes whether women are 20, 40, or 60 percent or more of the workers in the enterprise.

Another reason why Mr. Robie argues that management should revise its employment practices to increase the number of women in management positions is

that industry can simply no longer afford to waste so valuable a resource. As society expands and becomes more complex, so do the

[1] Edward A. Robie, "Challenge to Management," Eli Ginzberg and Alice M. Yohalem, eds., *Corporate Lib: Women's Challenge to Management* (Baltimore: The Johns Hopkins University Press, 1973), p. 10.

problems of the organizations serving it. Every available source of talent must be tapped if we are to cope effectively and competitively with these problems. It is entirely possible—I would even say probable—that women represent a source of superior talent to the company that can successfully recruit them. . . .[2]

Frankly, I cannot help but be rather amused at the whole notion that management is now going to turn to women because the problems of today's world have become too complex for men alone to solve. Such a new-found humility is a bit hard to believe, for regardless of whether our society would have done better with the managerial talents of women, it has certainly managed, up to now, to function without these talents. Why it should take the complexities of today's world to make men in positions of authority turn to women as an additional source of talent is something of a mystery—especially when utilizing these talents may seem to involve so many organizational problems and the disruption of traditional modes of behavior.

Continuing high rates of unemployment make it even more unlikely, of course, that a spontaneous desire to bring women into management will occur. Thus, while I believe that women do constitute a reserve of unused and undeveloped talents, I do not really believe this will be a powerful factor motivating employers to give them jobs. Frankly, I believe that if they do expand the opportunities for women in management it will be because they have to—because pressures will continue to mount for a more equalitarian sex distribution in jobs. And by pressures, I don't mean violent radical groups taking to the ramparts, burning bras and the like, but the usual sorts of pressures—through the courts and by means of new laws enforced by various governmental agencies.

I would like to explain why I think these pressures to admit women into men's occupations will continue. My comments will not be from the perspective of someone involved in the women's movement and hence in applying these pressures, nor even from the perspective of a social scientist studying the women's movement. Rather, my perspective is that of a sociologist-demographer

[2] Ibid., pp. 11–12.

involved in the analysis of female labor force participation. It seems to me that a greater familiarity with the changes that have occurred in female labor force participation will help us understand why pressures for the expansion of job opportunities for women are not likely to be a passing fad. Let me begin by reviewing some of the overall trends.

The extent of women's contribution to the national economy has changed considerably over the past ten years. The change has been particularly great since 1940 which marked the beginning of an accelerated growth in women's labor force participation. So great has this growth been that by 1970, 50 percent of American women aged 18 to 64 were in the labor force compared with 30 percent in 1940 and 20 percent in 1900.

Even more impressive is the changing relationship between female labor force participation and the family life cycle. In fact, this latter change overshadows the increase in the work rates for women as a whole. In 1900, if the average woman worked at all during her lifetime—and not a great many did—it was before marriage and children. A very small proportion were working later on in life. By 1940, the rates showed some changes in the *degree* of labor force participation, but the *pattern* by age was very similar to that of 1900. At both dates the peak work rates were among women in their early twenties and labor force participation declined sharply thereafter, never to rise again.

Starting sometime in the 1940s, however, there began to be a growing break with this traditional pattern of female labor force participation. The first great departure was the entrance or return of women past the age of 35 into the labor force—women whose children, by and large, had reached school age. Census data show a sharp increase between 1940 and 1950 in the work rates of women in the 35 to 64 age group. Furthermore, this pattern has persisted to this day—so much so that in 1970 between 49 and 54 percent of women between 35 and 59 years of age were in the labor force!

A second trend, starting in the 1950s but picking up considerable steam since 1960, has been the increased labor force participation of younger married women, including women with

33

pre-school children. The 1940 work rates for married women between 20 and 34 years of age indicate that at that time work was
a rather rare occurrence. The peak rate was for 20- to 24-year-
old women, yet only 26 percent of them were in the labor force.
However, by 1970, the Census reports work rates that ranged
from a low of 38 percent for women aged 25 to 29 to a high of 47
percent for women aged 20 to 24. There were striking increases
in the work rate of wives with preschool children, as well as of
childless wives and those with older children.

As a consequence, in 1970, just under one third of mothers
with preschoolers were working and 49 percent of mothers of
school age children were in the labor force. In sum, work is becoming an increasingly important part of women's entire lives,
not just during the period before they marry and start raising
children. In other words, the presence of children, whatever their
age, is becoming less and less of a deterrent to female labor
force participation.

Now, there is very little reason to believe that these increases
in female labor force participation are occurring because American women suddenly became uppity and decided they wanted to
have that grand thing, a career with a capital C. On the contrary,
studies in the mid-1960s of the potentially most career-minded
group—college students—indicate that very few girls planned to
have careers. Moreover, the kinds of jobs most working women
hold certainly do not fall into the career category. Rather, to
date, women's increased labor force participation seems to be
largely a product of two main factors—a considerable postwar
growth in the demand for female workers, that is, increasing job
opportunities for women, coupled with women's desire to raise
their families' standard of living. An indication of the latter is the
continuing influence of the size of a husband's income upon his
wife's decision to work and the increasing labor force participation of mothers whose husbands' incomes cannot keep up with
that most devastating of combinations—rising aspirations coupled
with rising inflation.

As a consequence of these trends many American families are
becoming increasingly dependent on the incomes of two earners

rather than on the earnings of the husband alone. To the extent that this situation becomes even more common, it cannot help but have an effect on women's job aspirations. For if women at all stages of the family life cycle are working in ever greater numbers, it is inevitable that many are going to stop viewing work as a brief interlude in a long life devoted to their families. Instead, they will start to look upon work as a possible lifetime activity, interrupted at times, perhaps, but nevertheless one of their major adult roles.

Thus, it is unlikely that women will continue to be satisfied with the kinds of jobs that used to be good enough for an interim period. As long as work was of secondary importance, women's work goals remained limited and the characteristics of women's jobs that make them most unattractive to men—poor pay and poor advancement opportunities—did not cause a great deal of dissatisfaction. However, as work becomes more important to women, and to their families as well, the more irritating will become the poor pay and the lack of opportunities so typical of female jobs.

Dissatisfaction with women's traditional occupations is likely to grow among all women workers but will be particularly acute among women who do not have the financial benefits derived from having a husband within the home, namely, the divorced and separated, whose economic welfare often depends entirely or very extensively on their own earning capacities. For many of these women a broken marriage coupled with their own low earning potential consigns them to a lifetime of economic marginality, not to mention the adverse effect of lowered incomes on the education of their children.

The situation is further aggravated by rising divorce rates and by the fact that a divorced woman's chances of remarriage are considerably less than those of a divorced man. As a consequence, the number of divorced and separated women rose 30 percent between 1960 and 1970, from 3.9 to 5 million, while the number of divorced men who did not remarry rose only 23 percent.

There are two other trends that will intensify the pressures for

35

women to break away from traditional female jobs. These are the rising educational attainment of American women and the decline from the very high fertility of the postwar baby boom period. Both of these trends can be expected to have a multiplicity of effects on female labor force participation and on the increasing pressure for an expansion in job opportunities for women.

While there is considerable debate as to just how much our fertility is declining, there is little doubt that—for the present, at least—birth rates are considerably below those of the 1950s and early 1960s. With regard to educational attainment, there has been a substantial increase in the proportion of women completing high school and the proportions entering and finishing college. As a result, the percent of very poorly educated women has declined sharply. Now what are some of the implications of these trends?

One important effect of a lowered birth rate is that it is likely to increase the number of women who want to work. This is because children still remain an important deterrent to female labor force participation in spite of the fact that they don't deter quite as much as they used to. Lowered fertility will, therefore, probably increase the number of women competing for the traditionally female jobs. This competition is likely to be considerably aggravated by the rising educational level of women and other consequences of the fertility decline.

As far as education is concerned, the increased proportion of women with a college degree will mean a rising demand for high level jobs. College women—quite understandably—have not been very interested in clerical work, much less in the poorly paid blue-collar female occupations. Their main job opportunities have been in the female professions, primarily teaching. Thus in 1970, 80 percent of women with four or more years of college were in the professions. However, with declining fertility, the school age population will not be expanding so opportunities for female employment in elementary and secondary education will not be on the rise. Furthermore, the decline of the female college, or at least its lack of expansion, means that a traditional source of jobs for women with graduate degrees may also be drying up.

Thus, at a time when the number of highly educated women is on the rise, the traditional source of jobs for such women is not expanding and may even be contracting. While some of these women may marry prosperous husbands and not need or care to work, many are going to want to work and I doubt whether they will be satisfied with the lower level professional and clerical jobs that may be open to them. These women are well-educated and verbal and often quite knowledgeable about how things get done in this world. Personally I do not think they will quietly fade out of the job market when things get rough. In my opinion, they are going to make a fuss—in fact they have already started to do just that.

Another factor that is likely to aggravate the job situation for women is that an increase in female educational attainment does not mean only an increase in the proportion of well-educated women but also means a decline in the poorly educated and a rise in the moderately educated. As a consequence, an increasing proportion of women workers from a broad socioeconomic spectrum are squeezing into the clerical job market. Although the proportion of all employed women who were clerical workers rose considerably in the 1960–70 period (from 25 to 35 percent), the rise was particularly marked for wives of blue-collar workers. For example, the proportion of wives of craftsmen and foremen employed in clerical occupations rose from 31 to 35 percent; for operatives' wives the rise was from 24 to 29 percent; and even for laborers' wives there was an increase from 14 percent in 1960 to 21 percent in 1970. In spite of the rapid postwar expansion in job opportunities in clerical work, it is hard to see how such occupations can continue to provide most of the job opportunities for the increasing number of female high school graduates being produced by our society. If office automation should cut into the demand for clerical workers in the 1970s and 80s, the job situation for women will be even more difficult.

To sum up, my point is that a rapid postwar increase in job

opportunities for women in the traditional female occupations has served to partially transform the economic role of women in the family. To the extent that this transformation is taking place, and to the extent that work is becoming an important role for mature women, women's job aspirations are bound to rise. The rising aspirations will be intensified by women's rising educational attainment. Yet at the same time that aspirations are on the rise, it is unlikely that the traditional female occupations can continue to provide the jobs necessary to maintain women's changing economic role. Moreover, in the case of the higher level female occupations, most notably teaching, the job opportunities are actually likely to shrink rather than expand in the foreseeable future at least. As a consequence, there will be increasing pressure on the part of women to break away from traditional female jobs into male jobs at all levels. But the pressure to enter male occupations is likely to be the greatest, I suspect, with respect to men's occupations at the highest levels because the traditional female job market for college women is exceedingly unlikely to expand nearly as much as is the population of college educated women who would like to work.

Some men may secretly think that an imminent job squeeze for women is about to send them back into the home—"where they belong." I would like to suggest that they think again for even with women's current low wages, the two-earner family has considerably more purchasing power than the single-earner family. From an economic point of view, there is little doubt that the working wife is good business.

4

Like Their Fathers Instead

Rosemary Park

I have chosen this title not to be cute but to express as succinctly as possible the thought that any resolution of the topic *Women's Challenge to Management* will involve some fundamental, but by no means impossible, changes in our traditional concepts of women's place. Girls might grow up like their fathers instead if we were sure what the model father and model mother were today. In Victorian times there was some certainty about these matters as indeed there was about the British empire. Within the family, as well as in that empire, power has shifted from clear concentration in the head to a new form which provides for participation, if not control by the natives. The time is therefore propitious to examine some of the possibilities now apparent which did not exist for women when Professor Higgins by teaching Eliza proper English opened to her a whole new spectrum of opportunities. Things turned out well for Eliza, who was an exception. Just before her time, however, in 1854, the English records show that of 80,000 women married, 68,000 were unable to sign their names in the registry.[1] In the matter of literacy

[1] Margaret Maison, "Insignificant Objects of Desire," *The Listener*, vol. 86, no. 2208 (July 22, 1971), p. 106.

alone great progress has been made in the intervening century and a quarter. But we are concerned today not with such elementary competences but with the opportunities for women whose education matches men's.

The title of this volume has been interpreted primarily to mean women's challenge to nonacademic management. I believe that some attention should also be paid to that unique form of corporation, the academic corporation. My own career has been in the management of education, but I have been fortunate in having a chance now to return to full-time university teaching, and can testify to both the administrative and the faculty experience as it involves women. In neither area are women fairly represented. Half of the women who graduate from college go into teaching, primarily below the college level.[2] Only 9 percent of all full professors are women, concentrated largely in the fields of education and social work.[3] A girl who wishes to do graduate work in history, political science, or sociology, for example, will find, in some distinguished graduate schools, no women who have attained this rank.[4] In other universities women may be 2, 3, or occasionally 4 percent of the total full professorial rank. To make the point clear, in the academic year 1923–24, 2.6 percent of the full professors on the Berkeley campus of the University of California were women. In the academic year 1969–70, 2.3 percent of the full professors on the Berkeley campus of the University of California were women. In actual numbers, there were three women in 1923–24; in 1969–70, there were 15.[5] Thus, history seems to indicate that

[2] John K. Folger et al., *Human Resources and Higher Education* (New York: Russell Sage Foundation, 1970), p. 9.

[3] Edith Green, "Unreasoning Prejudice," *Delta Kappa Gamma Bulletin*, Fall 1970, p. 13. See also "Higher Education and National Affairs," American Council on Education (Washington, D.C., July 17, 1970), p. 5.

[4] *Report of Committee on Status of Women*, American Historical Association, November 9, 1970; Victoria Schuck, "Some Comparative Statistics on Women in Political Science and Other Social Sciences," *Political Science*, Summer 1970, pp. 357 ff.; Alice S. Rossi, "Women and Professional Advancement," *Science*, 166 (Oct. 17, 1969): 356.

[5] *The Chronicle of Higher Education*, Feb. 9, 1970, pp. 2–5. See also *Report of the Subcommittee on the Status of Academic Women on the Berkeley Campus*, Academic Senate Office (Berkeley, Calif., 1970).

women had their feet in the door in the 1920s, but they never managed or chose to enlarge the opening.

Should a girl aspire to administrative rather than professorial responsibility in a college or university, she will find even fewer models. When I first became a college president, I was one of six feminine colleagues in a group of ten women college presidents who used to meet for regular discussion of our problems. Today only three of those ten positions are held by women and two of the incumbents have recently announced their resignations. Further, when I retired as vice chancellor at the University of California in Los Angeles, I was the only woman at that level in the university system, and as far as I know there is still no other female vice chancellor.

The university differs from the corporation in that a decision by a chief executive officer is not effective down through the ranks. The internal power structure of the university is really not vertical. It isn't quite horizontal, but there are horizontal aspects to it. For instance, the effective power to appoint members of the faculty lies largely with the faculty, that is, with the full professors. In other words, policy changes in the university, to be effective, must be supported by a consensus of the departments, and in these departments, one often finds extraordinary rigidity and resistance to change which serve to deter female appointments.

Yet if one looks first at the educational preparation of men and women at the collegiate level by examining the curricula at most colleges for women, it would be difficult indeed to say in what respect they differ from programs offered to men in the male institutions. There may be a few more courses in economics and mathematics for the males, but in both types of colleges the courses in history, English, fine arts, and natural science are comparable, as are those in language and social science. More men than women will select mathematics and economics as a major field and more women than men will choose languages. If the small deviations can be called skewing, it is important to bear in mind that it results not from any prescription of the institution but from individual decision, which no doubt reflects other factors than the kind of education actually *offered* the two sexes. In the coeducational institutions courses and majors are obviously the same at both graduate and undergraduate level. The absence of women, then, in the higher echelons of professional life cannot, I think, be attributed to the *substance* of their college studies.

In overall grade point average the girls are somewhat superior to the boys. At commencement in 1970, 90.2 percent of the Radcliffe senior class graduated with honors as compared with 73.3 percent of the Harvard class.[6] These grades, one must remember, were given by the same faculty. Differences may be less dramatic in other institutions, but the girls' records are more than adequate testimony to their capacity to do the same college work as the boys—a matter once hotly contested when higher education was first opened to women in the middle and last half of the nineteenth century.

Once women had educational opportunity offered them, it would be natural to suppose that substantial numbers of women graduates would appear in the professions and in public and economic life. As we know, this has not taken place, and one could surmise that something must have happened to Little Red Riding Hood on her way to the forum and the agora. What was it? The simplest and the traditional answer has been that in spite of her degree she didn't want to go there in the first place. She wanted to marry and raise a family, which society concurred in urging her to do as her first and unique responsibility. Through most of history it has been assumed that this assignment requires a lifetime of exclusive devotion and that it could be exercised as well without a college degree as with one.

No one doubts that American women college graduates are prepared educationally and on intellectual grounds to enter the professions. That not many do is only partly attributable to overt discrimination. The motivational factors which account for able women settling for jobs rather than careers are complex. "What is a pretty girl like you doing in a chemistry lab, an economics class, or a graduate school?" This question represents the

[6] Radcliffe College, "News from the College," Cambridge, Mass., Summer 1970.

folk wisdom on the matter, and the message is reinforced in countless ways by parents, by school counselors, and by the media, not to mention the family service consultants and the popular interpreters of modern psychological theory. All of these seem to be arguing the old dichotomy, marriage versus career. Valid as this may once have been, and the lives of the "dedicated spinsters" remind us of that truth, the facts do not support this difficult choice as real in the lives of most women today. Both the marriage rate and the rate of female employment continue to rise. One study projects only a 3 percent unmarried group among women reaching middle age in the 1980s.[7] However, the age at marriage appears to be increasing somewhat and this may mean more education and even better preparation for employment.

Before accepting this as a possible trend toward more ambitious employment plans, there are other factors to be considered. Joseph Katz is quoted in the *Chronicle of Higher Education* as saying, "Our educational system encourages women to high performance and strong intellectual achievement but only until they graduate from college. Then social, economic, and educational arrangements make it difficult if not impossible to continue these interests." Bruno Bettelheim has pointed to the contrast in educational motivation for the boy and the girl: he acquires an education to enable him to succeed; she sees hers as a defense against failure to marry.[8] This negative attitude is clearly demonstrated in a finding of the *California Commission on the Status of Women*, which reported in 1969 that, of a representative sample of teenage girls questioned, 42 percent were not sure that they would be successful in their chosen field.[9] The American Council on Education's study of entering freshmen showed, as late as the fall of 1967, that about half of the freshmen women planned no degree higher than the B.A., while for only 27 percent

[7] Cynthia Fuchs Epstein, *Woman's Place: Options and Limits in Professional Careers* (Berkeley: University of California Press, 1970), p. 94.

[8] Ibid., p. 64. See also Eli Ginzberg, *Life Styles of Educated Women* (New York: Columbia University Press, 1966), pp. 166 ff.

[9] See *Los Angeles Times*, May 25, 1969.

43

of the men was this first degree to be terminal. Women intending to study for the doctorate or equivalent professional degrees represented 12 percent of the female group compared to 36 percent of the male sample.[10] These figures are measures of aspiration, not achievement or even commitment, but they help to explain why it is that the proportion of females awarded doctor's degrees has declined. Apparently strong motivation for career training is not established among American young women.

Anyone who has ever tried to raise money for women's colleges knows that familiar deflating response to your appeal, "They will only get married anyway!" Whether the women's college had an adequate library, science laboratory, or gymnasium, these were matters of indifference to the possible philanthropist. Fortunately, being a unique collection of personalities, philanthropists occasionally include a variant who is as concerned for women's education as for men's. But for one such, there have been too many others, except for widows of the wealthy, who have given only to the man's college, sure in their conviction that women did not need higher education. Even the contributions of alumnae to their alma maters seldom equal the sums raised by the alumni of the male institutions. Some improvement has been noted sporadically in the last years.

This, then, would be an easy place to stop, and many people do, concluding that marriage and homemaking have always been the exclusive preoccupation and occupation of women and that, while higher education is pleasant enough for a woman to have had, like the drawing and singing her great grandmother was taught, it does not supply an essential dimension to a woman's life as it does to a man's. The matter could rest there with only a few atypical women entering professions and employment. And indeed from some points of view this is an acceptable resolution of the problem. Cynthia Epstein in her recent book *Woman's Place* remarks, "Women who have chosen careers in elite professions are as deviant . . . in 1968 as they were in 1898."[11]

[10] *A Fact Book on Higher Education*, American Council on Education, Washington, D.C., 3 (1968): 8163.
[11] Epstein, *Woman's Place*, p. 6.

Despite conventional assumptions, however, the matter cannot rest there today because while Red Riding Hood did not emerge at the top she didn't stay home either. If the agora has a ground floor, that is where Red Riding Hood went when she did not go directly home with her college diploma, or so it would seem.

However, the present outline of women's participation in economic life appears to be one of initiation, withdrawal, and return. The clustering of females in the lower echelons of professions and occupations could be explained as a result of this interesting pattern, especially in occupations or professions where specialized techniques or research findings are being daily incorporated into the practice of the fields, resulting in constant change. An instance is reported of a fully qualified woman being refused a position because the appointing officer opined that she could not keep up with the literature in the field if her household duties were going to require a portion of her evening hours.[12] For women in less demanding types of employment where there is no necessity to keep up with the field, this pattern is clearly a live option. Relating the continuing increase in women employees to unemployment in 1970, the Women's Bureau of the U.S. Department of Labor said, "If all women stayed home and the unemployed men were placed in the jobs held by women, there would be 29.3 million unfilled jobs."[13] In addition, the women not presently in the labor force because they have not yet returned constitute a reserve pool, at least theoretically, which could be drawn upon in emergency conditions.

This pattern of withdrawal and return, however, can have negative effects. If generalized as the norm, it would tend to confine women to the lower strata of employment. This direction and the tendency to underpay women for equal work could delay the development of professional attitudes toward work. Nevertheless the fact that more and more women are living in this withdraw-and-return pattern despite its advantages means

[12] Anne G. Pannell, "Is the New Woman New Enough?" *Graduate Comment* [Wayne State University], vol. 12, no. 1 (1969): 49.

[13] U.S. Department of Labor, Women's Bureau, *Background Facts on Women Workers in the United States* (Washington, D.C., 1970), p. 4.

that it is a genuine alternative to lifelong homemaking and one which management can count on to persist unless an anti-Freud arises who calls in question present childrearing customs with their emphasis on a close association in the early years for the healthy development of both mother and child.

I have already commented on the paucity of women in the upper ranks of college administration and faculty. To some extent, this may be accounted for by absence from the profession for childbearing during the crucial years of academic development as Alice Rossi and others have suggested.[14] But this explanation can only hold for women who have chosen this life style of withdrawal and return. Today there are, as there have been for the last century at least, women who are seeking a genuine professional career on the basis of interest, capacity, and training. A generation ago such women were found in numbers among the faculty and administrators of the women's colleges. These dedicated spinsters, however, have almost disappeared as the number of unmarried American women has steadily decreased.

It may be significant that the proportion of doctorates awarded women has also decreased. In 1930 women earned 15.4 percent of all doctor's degrees granted and in 1966 11.6 percent, which represents a slight increase over the proportion given to women in 1960 which was 10.5 percent.[15] It is only fair to observe, however, that though the proportion declined, there was nevertheless an increase in the actual number of women doctorates. This increase has not provided American career women with the kind of visibility, however, which women professionals in other countries enjoy.

Most of us are familiar with the contrast between the proportionate number of American women physicians and Russian, 6.5 percent as compared with 75 percent. Similar discrepancies exist in science—38 percent of all Russian scientists are women, 7

[14] Alice S. Rossi, "Women in Science: Why So Few," *Science*, 148 (May 28, 1965): 1196 ff.

[15] Epstein, *Woman's Place*, p. 58.

46

percent of American. In Denmark 70 percent of all dentists are women, in America 2.1 percent.[16] Less dramatic but significant differences are found in other fields requiring graduate preparation. It may be objected that Denmark and Russia define the professional responsibilities of doctors and dentists somewhat differently from America. These important functions in society are nevertheless being filled by competent women more often than by men, and in other professional areas women are better represented than in America. Since there is no evidence that American women are less able, one is forced to conclude that they are subject either to widespread discrimination or to most effective brainwashing which prevents many gifted women from aspiring to actual participation in professional life. Studies to date seem to indicate that both assumptions are valid.

Eve Merriam has been quoted as saying, "Sex prejudice is the only prejudice now considered socially acceptable." Like some other prejudices this one too may be found among quite intelligent people. Lawrence Simpson's study of employing agents' attitudes toward academic women has shown that men under 30 or over 60 are least prejudiced.[17] A more recent study, "Women in Academia," by A. Y. Lewin and Linda Duchan,[18] tends to reinforce the evidence about the older men and supports the lack of prejudice among younger men under some conditions. The general conclusion reached, however, is similar to most other examinations of discrimination against women. Namely, "the data yielded consistently a trend in the direction of the existence of discrimination against women in academic life."

The same study suggests that different criteria may be used in evaluating the female candidate. In general these criteria may not be strictly related to training and ability but rather to tem-

[16] Ibid., p. 12.
[17] Lawrence A. Simpson, "Attitudes of Higher Education Employing Agents Toward Academic Women," *Graduate Comment*, p. 41.
[18] A. Y. Lewin and Linda Duchan, "Women in Academia," *Science*, 173 (Sept. 3, 1971): 892–95.

perament and to social pressures and family responsibilities. To some extent this type of discrimination arises out of the uneasiness caused by a foreigner in a group of natives. The club was much nicer before we admitted Jews and blacks and now women. Reasons are sought to justify exclusion. In the case of women, for example, absenteeism will be cited, even though a recent Department of Labor bulletin quotes a public health survey showing absentee rate for illness or injury for women at 5.9 days compared with 5.2 days for men per year.[19]

A psychologist has related this desire for masculine exclusiveness to a need, instinctive with the male, for bonding. Lionel Tiger remarks that "it can be argued that male bonding was preadaptive, possibly part of man's primate endowment."[20] If this is indeed so, then women have a fearsome task if their participation at the top echelons of professions and public life is going to run counter to a prehistoric necessity of the male to hunt in packs whether the prey be beasts, a foreign trade contract, the double helix, or an election.

Rather than leave the problem of sex prejudice to be explained as a vestigial urge in the American male to associate himself only with other males in the attainment of interesting objectives, I should like to follow a different line of inquiry which arises from the concept of sex-typed occupations. Much of what appears to be sex prejudice is masked by the contention that women do not belong in this particular activity but do quite well in another one where they dominate. Robert Merton and others have shown that sex-typing of occupations tends to take place where numerical dominance by one sex is associated with a normative expectation that this dominance *should* prevail in the occupation in question.[21] Interpreted, this means that everyone agrees it is fine for a woman to be a school teacher or a nurse, a social worker or librarian, all occupations in which women

[19] U.S. Department of Labor, *Women's Bureau Bulletin*, April 1971, p. 1.
[20] Lionel Tiger, *Men in Groups* (New York: Random House, Inc., 1969), p. 96.
[21] Epstein, *Woman's Place*, p. 152.

predominate. It is not suitable, however, for women to be engineers, bankers, or lawyers, where they have but the scantiest representation now.

The time, of course, is still within the memory of man when most teachers were men, social workers had not been invented, and nurses were both male and female, having evolved from the charitable activities of the various medieval religious orders. In our own time, however, these occupations are clearly stamped in the public mind as female occupations. No clearer proof could be found than the fact that not until 1966 did the United States permit *male* nurses to hold commissions in the Army, Navy, and Air Force Nurse Corps.[22] As early as 1871 Prime Minister Gladstone questioned these stereotype divisions of labor when he said in the House of Commons, "I scarcely ever see in the hands of a woman an employment that ought more naturally to be in the hands of a man, but I constantly see in the hands of a man employment which might be more beneficially and economically in the hands of a woman."[23] Like most stereotypes sex-typing of occupations tends to be a self-fulfilling prophecy. The more women in the occupation, the fewer men apply; and as a result women monopolize all openings, and it becomes a woman's occupation, which is apt to have discriminatory pay scales and to lack the honorific nature of most of men's professions.

Both history and cross-cultural observations show that sex-typing is subject to limited validity. If medicine is clearly typed as a woman's profession in Russia and dentistry as a woman's profession in Denmark, then American reluctance to encourage women in these fields is purely capricious. Its persistence may be a form of sex prejudice which uses the rationalization of sex-typed professions to hide a deeper and irrational discrimination against women. It is salutary in this regard that the *Encyclopaedia Britannica*, as recently as the eleventh edition, contains a strong plea for male nurses because, among other grounds, "it is

[22] Quoted from *New York Times*, August 16, 1966, in ibid., p. 153.
[23] Quoted in Tiger, *Men in Groups*, p. 81.

excessively irksome to a sensitive man to be attended by women for various necessary offices. In order to avoid it he will endeavor to do without assistance and seriously prejudice his chances of recovery."[24] The sentiment, if not the detail, has a familiar ring.

Again one could conclude at this point by expressing the hope that in an age when so many bastions of prejudice are collapsing, this particular form of discrimination will cease to be effective and that women will gradually be permitted freedom to exercise their talents as their training, industry, and aspirations indicate. Such social change requires, of course, time. Other minority groups have refused to accept the slow modification of social consciousness as assurance of eventual justice. Women, I think, may be permitted a similar impatience. The reports of various manpower surveys show all too clearly that the situation in sex-typed professions may shortly result in an even more drastic curtailment of women's participation in economic life than in the past, and that therefore deceleration of discrimination is in order. John Folger's *Human Resources and Higher Education* indicates that by 1980 only 12 to 14 percent of the college graduates will be required in elementary and secondary teaching compared to half of all women college graduates who entered the profession in the 1950s and 1960s.[25] Of the apparent excess some, of course, could enter activities related to education, research and counseling for example. If present sex stereotypes regarding professions persist, however, it will be difficult to attract women and for women to enter other professions where the need may be greater for trained personnel than in teaching.

Fortunately there is some evidence that discrimination in the form of sex typing is breaking down. Dr. Harold Kaplan of New York Medical College is quoted in the *Los Angeles Times* for September 12, 1971, as saying that "throughout the world, medicine is becoming a woman's field and I believe it will happen here too." He also reports that at the moment only South Vietnam, Madagascar, and Spain have a smaller proportion of

[24] *Encyclopaedia Britannica*, 11th ed. (1911), 19: 917.
[25] Folger, *Human Resources*, p. 9.

women doctors than does the United States. The shifting of manpower requirements and a weakening of overt and covert discrimination may indeed open other professions to women who wish careers in the immediate future. It has always been conceded that individuals with outstanding talent can break out of the stereotype. There have been in the past and there are now in America distinguished women doctors, lawyers, and professors. In the age of the common man, however, we are not concerned with what an atypical individual can do but with what society will offer and approve for the group. This approval needs to be more easily accorded women.

Even though overt restriction fades, in the case of women the level of feminine aspiration itself remains a deterrent as effective as discrimination itself in shaping feminine lifestyles. The suggested existence of a phenomenon called male bonding was mentioned in connection with the sex-typing of professions. No similar female-associated impulse seems to exist. Women's organizations to advance certain causes are rarely large. Even women's lib presents no united front, and surely part of its effectiveness is due to the climate of opinion created by the emergence of organized racial groups into American life. Just as they are attaining through more radical tactics a justice they would have still had to wait for, so the time is ripe to study the disabilities which society imposes and women accept and which tend to prevent their planning and training for more adventurous living. It is unlikely, however, that women will unite in advancing this claim. David Riesman and others have commented on the inability of women to form an autonomous subculture, except, as Riesman says, in the convent.[26]

It is by no means self-evident that America needs women, or more women than at present, to train themselves to their highest capacity in order to serve the country in some way. Neither, of course, is it obvious that America needs black lawyers, bankers, and managers from any purely economic stand-

[26] David Riesman, "Dilemmas of the Educated—Especially Women," *Pitzer College Bulletin*, vol. 7, no. 2 (Sept. 1969).

point. We have nevertheless agreed that this will be a less good country without this minority participation, and we are prepared to encourage training to this end. We need perhaps to see the participation of women as a similar attempt to improve the quality of American life by removing obstacles to full self-development. The racial minorities are aided in their demands by organized group pressure from the minority itself. Women will not unite in their cause because there are at least two other life styles opened to them, full and lifetime marriage and homemaking or the withdraw-and-return pattern without special ambition beyond equal pay. The counseling most girls receive in school and the parental environment will all suggest one of these two styles. It will still be hard for the girl who wants to have a career to find much but put-downs and no-no's to her ambition, at least in the current climate of unemployment, discrimination, and sex-typed professions.

What can the university do to help here? I do think that we have been particularly remiss in not giving support to those women whose ability and desires warrant much more meaningful professional activity, whether it be in academic life, in business or in the professions. Many schools have experimented with courses for women directed to what we concede to be the problems of women, and I think these probably are useful, particularly where they are open to both men and women. There I think one sees more clearly that the problems we are dealing with here are societal problems, and that they are not just misunderstandings between the sexes. The usefulness of these courses, as I have seen them, has been to stretch the empathy for women's role. I know of one instance where an experimental course had been set up and when the question arose as to whether it would be added to the standard curriculum, the students who came to testify before the committee about its importance were all boys who said they never had realized the extent or nature of women's problems and that they thought more of their fellow students should be exposed to such classes.

However, while something can be accomplished this way, I do not think that this does enough to stretch the ambition of able women. They, I think, need models whose lives are presented through the media and elsewhere as not being simply ones of austere devotion to some kind of homing instinct, but as lives of vitality, excitement, and fulfillment because of activity that uses the full capacity of the personality.

I suppose the most important and the most difficult aspect of this problem is to get the faculty to recognize that indeed there is a problem. This is peculiarly true of women faculty who have made it. They seem to forget that there were many women who didn't make it and that they didn't make it, perhaps, because they were not as tough or because they didn't have the good fortune to be encouraged along the way.

If one is speaking with men faculty, then I think the problem is even perhaps more acute because you have the difficulty of showing them that there is indeed a problem, and that it isn't just a question of patting someone on the back and giving encouragement. Unless there is a greater sensitivity on the part of many faculty members that a little encouragement where warranted and a stretching of the ambition of the girls is necessary, I don't think the universities will have discharged their responsibility.

Earlier I mentioned the relative lack of prejudice against women among academic administrators in the younger and older age brackets. It is interesting to speculate as to whether this openness on the part of younger executives is related in any way to the androgynous character of modern youth styles. Women have an important role in this new youth culture and it may be that the long haired, bead-wearing youth of today will be more sympathetic to women seeking careers than his predecessors. Since the youth revolution concerns itself with *being* more than *becoming*, it cannot be expected to encourage either men or women to aim high within the achieving society it rejects. At the moment this cultural movement appears to be a stage from which young people emerge with a more unselfish value system. They are faced nevertheless with a highly technological society which must be mastered on its own demanding terms. This does not mean that it cannot be modified to do greater justice to the need for self-realization of all minorities, among which I include

53

women who have the desire and the capacity to become professionals or to serve in the higher echelons of public and economic life.

Steps by management looking to increased opportunity for women as well as for racial minorities might well prove a genuine contribution toward the reduction of alienation between most executives and the younger generation. Just as there are plans for the recruitment of racial minorities, so there could well be attempts to develop administrative talent among women and a genuine effort could be made to modify old patterns of professional training to encourage women's participation. Whether temporary less than full-time job responsibility can permit a wife or her husband or both of them to assume child care responsibilities, there is not yet enough evidence to judge. Little information is available, partly because as the Society of Personnel Administrators discovered, 87 percent of companies have five percent or fewer women in management above the first line and academic opportunity is similarly restricted.[27] In both sectors stereotypes of women's behavior exist which effectively prevent recruitment. Women are said to be absent more than men, to change jobs more often, and to be hard to work with. All three of these charges persist despite valiant efforts of the Women's Bureau to defuse them. The challenge to management then is to try to be fair to the woman employee but more especially to experiment with some less than full-time positions for a possible three-year period while the married woman endeavors to play two parts at once, mother and executive. We have no way of knowing how many men would like to work less than the traditional full-time pattern because the question can hardly be asked. Just as custom binds women into sex-typed activities, so men are not perceived as anything but full-time employees. Otherwise they are obliged, like the woman lawyer or retailer, to explain why they do not fit the traditional image for their sex.

Throughout this discussion I have suggested that this tradi-

[27] Bureau of National Affairs, American Society for Personnel Administration, "Bulletin to Management," March 5, 1970.

tional image needs to be reexamined in the light of elementary justice. Although I have structured my argument to concern myself with women's deprivations, I am convinced that more flexible typing of professions and more imaginative scheduling of work would profit men as well as women. Demands for these changes may well come from the younger generation when they begin to participate in the leadership of society. A willingness to experiment with the conventional arrangements of employment may be the principal request to management, but it will be founded on the new insights which this very generous and idealistic generation cherishes. It would be farthest from their thoughts or mine that all women should have careers, or all men. Some nations have calculated the additive to the GNP if women were more fully employed. According to a Swedish economist quoted in the November 28, 1968, edition of the *Boston Globe*, "Swedish national income would be increased by some 25 percent if the unused labor potential of women were fully utilized." A French economist maintains that the standard of living in France "would rise by 35 percent if women were professionally active to the same extent as men." These extrapolations are interesting and possibly even true. They are, however, unlikely to move young Americans to try to make them the basis for a more just and more flexible interpretation of woman's role.

Women's challenge to management then is first to cooperate fully in enforcing all legal restrictions on discrimination and all aspects of equal pay requirements. Our technique in our university has been to secure the appointment of a senate or of a faculty committee to take on the task of assembling the data on female employment. I would call this the "shocking" data. They also made recommendations to their colleagues and are prepared, through them, finally to urge action upon the administration in those areas where something is required. The report on the status of women which was written on the Berkeley campus seems to me an excellent example of the kind of committee work which faculties can undertake.[28] Their committee consisted

[28] *Status of Academic Women on the Berkeley Campus.*

of three women and two men, and it made recommendations to the president of the university, to the chancellor of that campus, to committees of the Senate including the Budget Committee, the University Welfare Committee, the Committee on Committees, and the Graduate Council. They even made recommendations to the directors of the faculty clubs.

I mention this to indicate the diversity of interest and indeed of power which resides in the university structure. And I mention it further as an indication that without substantial consent among these areas of power, the university does not move. Further, it is an excellent example of the team approach to decisionmaking.

I suggest that the university may have learned something, even in a small way, that might be useful. I am not going to repeat all the recommendations of this Berkeley report but will give just a couple of examples. They recommended the abolition of antinepotism regulations "with appropriate procedural administrative rules to prevent conflict of interest." They also recommended paid maternity leave "with a maximum of two per woman."

They recommended aggressive recruitment programs and zero population growth. The recruitment programs should be financed by a specially established budget pool "with an ultimate goal of having a representation of qualified women faculty at each rank at least in rough proportion to the number of women trained in that field," that is, trained in the field at the University of California.

Now I believe that this was a good report. The speed of implementation, however, depends to a very large extent upon the heads of departments, and they are nothing short of intransigent. They very reluctantly pay attention to, let alone serve, any chancellor or president. However, they do watch the action of other department chairmen, and the head of a department in most universities today is not a permanent appointee in that position. Chairmanships rotate, and younger and more sensitive men are coming to have this responsibility, many of whom I know, by first hand acquaintance, are eager and anxious to

56

cooperate to make women's participation in faculties and in administration more commensurate with their capacity.

Once the problem is grasped by the university, once it is seen as a problem and not as a nonproblem, then it seems to me one can count on a genuine desire among many members of the academic community to correct the imbalance in the sex distribution aided in that noble reaction by government legislation.

I am also optimistic about the university situation because reports like these have very seldom been the work of women only. They have been the work of men and women, and this means to me that in solving this problem women will not necessarily be working *alone* but may be working together with men to form a life style that could be of advantage to both sexes.

I remember talking with a university president who recently instituted a coeducational program about the necessity of having part-time appointments for women on his faculty. He replied to me in some dismay that, if he had them for women, he would have to have them for men. And I said "Why not?" to which he did not reply.

The emergence of more successful women in top positions will expose discriminatory practices as inconsistent with women's abilities but will have the more important consequence that women will learn to think about their lives not in the short-term fashion of their mothers but in the longer-term like their fathers instead. Some women will choose the traditional pattern of home-making; some will choose or be obliged to enter employment without developing any special career interest; others will participate as equals in the professional and economic life of the country, but all will have made an informed choice. If present cultural revolutionary tendencies persist, we may find that men too will begin to lay claim to the same variety of life styles open to women. By making these styles all free and honorable, society will cultivate a greater richness and diversity among men and women than our traditions have yet permitted.

5

Brainwashed Women

Mary Sarah Fasenmyer

The first area I will address myself to is the responsibility of education in terms of the counseling of our young people. Dr. Park has stated in her paper, and I agree with her completely, that many women have been brainwashed and that the aspirations of girls are not realistic. I suggest that much of this kind of brainwashing—if that is the right word—begins in the home. But I also think it is inherent in our educational system. We talk about education as being a leader in social change, but we don't have much evidence for it. Education really reflects society rather than leads it, and this reflection is particularly evident in the counseling that is given to girls.

Most vocational counseling takes place in school. Those of us in schools of education which train counselors must recognize that we have, however inadvertently, contributed to the persistence of female stereotypes. We have a fairly large guidance department in our school of education at Catholic University and I have talked with my faculty about this particular problem. They agree that much vocational counseling that goes on now in the educational setting still presents girls with no other option than a choice between career and marriage.

I believe that schools of education and educators in general must do some soul searching in order to see how they can change female counseling. True, guidance does begin in the home, but if we really feel that education makes a difference, then we can perhaps successfully reverse negative family influences.

I think that the counseling of girls who are entering college also must change. For instance, in 1971, our own school of education, at the undergraduate level, had an increase in applicants for admission to the teacher education curriculum. In fact, five institutions with good teacher training courses in our metropolitan area all had increases in the students who wished to become teachers. I understand this was true elsewhere as well. I wonder whether encouraging such study is responsible guidance when so many new teachers could not get jobs this year and projections show that teacher demand is not going to improve. It seems to me that colleges have to take a very responsible posture in terms of guiding entering college women into fields where they can be productive and where they can make a contribution.

The second point I'd like to make in relation to the university is that we need to come up with some better standards of evaluation of performance at the higher levels. I have inquired about the criteria for evaluating men as potential candidates for managerial positions and have received very vague answers. We talk about effectiveness and we talk about efficiency, but we do not have any operational definitions that make sense.

Now in education, we talk a good deal about evaluation and accountability. We talk about competency, basic education, and a lot of terms that have never been clearly defined. Actually in higher education the method of evaluating performance is very weak. Most of it is done by colleagues, and most colleagues in higher education tend to be men who, it has been established, have a high level of prejudice. I would suggest that we need some stronger-based criteria by which women can be evaluated for admission to positions in the university and for movement up the ladder.

There is an interesting assumption that one hears when discussing entry levels and advancement up the ladder: that all of

59

the men on the job are competent and efficient. Nobody ever mentions the Peter Principle! It may have been a spoof on organizations, but I think there is evidence that it operates. I think that the assumption that all the men are competent is not really valid. Certainly, I question whether they are more competent than women at the same levels. I do feel that, once the women get into the lower ranks, if there is a viable base for evaluating them without regard to sex, they will make the grade and they will advance to the responsible levels that they should.

The third point I'd like to make is that within the higher educational unit I still believe very strongly that more of the responsibility should fall on the women who are already a part of it, the women professors and the students. Dr. Park does make a point in her paper that I might take exception to, and that is that women will not band together in their own interests. I would suggest that they haven't but that there are many cultural reasons that could indeed be the rationale for this. A quote from David Reisman struck home because he said that the only evidence that he finds of women banding together is in religious orders within the Catholic church, and I know about that! In fact, I can say a great deal about the phenomenon of women banding together in an extremely male-oriented bureaucratic organization which has been cited as the most effective and powerful bureaucracy in the world. I think the example simply shows that women *will* band together and that when conditions are ripe they do and are doing so now.

What happens on the campus? How do women indeed make their cause known? Dr. Park spoke about committee appointments, recognizing that a campus works by the committee system. I don't really know of any other way to make it work. Everything happens in the committee. Thus, women are automatically ineffectual if they are not placed on important committees.

Women on campus must make a determined effort to get their voices heard on committees. After they get there, it is up to them to make their impact. Like minorities, they have to overcompensate, to try harder. I think we do, and I think we will.

The next point I would make, in relation to the university, is concerned with the role of instruction. This is supposed to be the educators' chief arena, the chief domain of action. That which we are is that which we teach is a truism, and it is of some concern to me that we should be able to say it truthfully. The tremendous amount of discrimination that is practiced by men on campus is especially disturbing because they do most of the teaching. Either they are not practicing what they teach or they are reinforcing discriminatory attitudes through their teaching, as well as through their actions.

The teaching of social justice, I believe, could be happening and should be happening in our classrooms, and this means bringing it to the attention of the faculty. This is one of the units of society that has been most guilty of discrimination, and yet this is the unit of society that is trying to mold our young people of the future.

It is worth considering whether this is a reason why young people at the undergraduate level are so unresponsive to their college education. I think we, at the university level, have to examine many of our practices in relation to women students. For example, there is a great deal of evidence that women students are discriminated against in many ways in the classroom. Somehow, the women on the campus are going to have to be some kind of a catalyst in making their needs known. We made a quick study on our campus, and we found that the cost of educating the men was considerably more than for the women. This is true at the high school level, but there the cause for the difference is mainly athletics, which play a minor role for most males at the college level. The only thing that was more costly as far as women's education at the college level was concerned, in comparison with men's, was the cost of security. The expense of keeping dorms secure for the women was so high that it tended to balance all the other educational costs which were higher for men. But costs of security are quite clearly not totally valid educational costs.

Nevertheless, I do see a very definite change on the campus. When we look at the participation of youth in all the various kinds of campus activism, women are found very clearly among them. They seem to be playing just as vital a role as the men do. We see women in the kind of leadership roles on the coeducational campus that they never assumed before. If this participation is here now, and if it is accepted and welcomed and furthered, I would say that I feel very optimistic about change. It may not occur, but it is a very positive sign.

I would share Dr. Park's optimism that more women are and will be coming into the field of teaching at the university level. But I am concerned because more women are now approaching the doctorate at a time when they may be unable to find employment because of present economic conditions. Therefore the number of women who seek doctorates may decrease. Moreover, the lowered demand for persons with doctoral degrees is leading more men to seek and acquire principalships and other high echelon jobs in elementary and high schools to the disadvantage of women.

While I do not support job differentiation in terms of sex, I do believe that we must take heed of the fact that many, many women have not been able to get teaching jobs recently. In my metropolitan area men students who had completed teacher training were the ones who were able to get the few jobs rather than women. While I do not have any data, I have a personal hypothesis that as we have put more and more men into leadership roles in education in our elementary and secondary schools, there has been an increase in criticism of the educational system. This may be an example of feminine chauvinism, but it may also relate to administrative styles—or perhaps female resentment in lower echelons which may tend to sabotage school goals.

I would like to conclude my remarks by saying that I still strongly believe in the American system of education. We're putting a tremendous investment in education and will continue to do this. Our society apparently continues to believe in it. I continue to believe in it or I certainly would not be in my present position. If it is really true that education makes a difference, then I think that educators and observers should examine very closely the contribution that education can make to solving women's problems and society should look to education to play a major role in their solution.

6

An Economist's View of Women's Work

James W. Kuhn

I am not an expert on women's discrimination. I speak only as a father of four daughters, as a husband of a wife who works for pay lower than that of men doing exactly the same work, and also, perhaps most significantly in terms of my own feelings and emotions about it, as the son of a widowed mother who in the Depression had to earn a living in a man's world to support her young children.

I remember two incidents from my childhood that left a bitter taste in my mouth. My mother could not go back to teaching after my father died because at that time, in the very depths of the Depression, jobs in teaching were reserved for married men and for single women. A widow, despite her responsibilities as family head, was not considered eligible for such employment.

After eight years of menial jobs and maintaining a farm, she was awarded a postmastership, and I remember the talk among the neighbors that this was very unfair because other candidates for the job were men who had families. That my mother had a family, too, seems never to have occurred to any of them.

Dr. Park's picture of the arbitrary discrimination suffered by women in hiring and pay and promotion is, as far as I know, an accurate one. The details are well highlighted by facts and figures. It is a sorry picture. I would suggest, however, that we have accepted it for as long as we have and that we have not attempted to make changes because, however bad it is, it has served some kind of reasonable social function, perhaps an economic function as well.

Men found it necessary to discriminate against women and then rationalized their discrimination as desirable. Elizabeth Janeway in her book, which I highly recommend, *Man's World and Woman's Place*, reminds us that through most of history woman's place has not been in the home, since the home as we know it today hardly existed. Even in agrarian America, which dominated all of the United States until the 1920s and some areas until World War II, women did not simply serve their husbands and their children, tending the housekeeping chores, cooking meals, mending, and rearing children. They carried out those activities, but they did much more besides. They were *full* partners in the economic undertaking of the farm.

For example, they were the major suppliers of the family food. Last summer I went through some of my mother's letters from the 1920s and earlier and through some of my grandmother's autobiography. What impressed me more than anything else was the enormous amount of work they performed: raising cash crops, preserving, tending and harvesting the garden, raising chickens, and selling produce. In fact, I came to the conclusion that the major portion of the family food came from women's work and effort. The wife on the farm helped not only in providing the food but also in various other farm routines: milking cows, harvesting fruit or vegetable crops and helping to pack them for the market, helping to manage harvest hands and to oversee their work, and acting as paymaster and foreman.

Adult women in the past were expected to work through the whole of their adult lives, and they did. Indeed from my own background, farming would not and could not have provided any family with the sustaining income that it did without the aid and contributions that the women provided.

Industrialization gradually pulled women away from the farm.

At first, they worked only part-time, in the shops and the mills and the factories, adding a small cash income to the returns of the farm. Later, when the families left the farm to move near the city or town, the wife was left with the children to tend for there was no new economically significant work to replace her accomplishments on the farm. The result is that the nation now has a large sector of the population, mostly women, who cannot easily find socially useful and satisfying employment.

The numbers may be far larger than our unemployment figures suggest. During the average week in 1970, 31½ million women were in the labor force, that is, more than 43 percent of all women 16 years old and over. About 1.8 million of these women were unemployed. However, during the entire year, there were 39 million women, or 52½ percent of the females in this age group, who worked for some period of time. Over 4 million of these women had one or more spells of unemployment, more than twice the number unemployed in the average week.

Thus, it seems likely that a considerable number of women who ordinarily do not work regularly would do so if work were available. If these women were added to our unemployment figures, the unemployment rate would be substantially higher than at present. I therefore wonder if Marx's industrial reserve army may not be more of a reality than we have ordinarily recognized. Our labor force accounting doesn't record this female reserve because of the peculiar way we define unemployment. But it may exist there, hidden from our national data, in the form of underutilized and unused women.

If we go back a hundred years to 1870 and look at this kind of problem, we find that at the time 53 percent of our labor force was gainfully employed on the farm. Only one out of every six workers was in manufacturing. Shortly after that, in the next two decades, technological change swept through the agricultural sector. The horse rake did the work of seven men with hand rakes; the mower replaced ten men with scythes; the reaper accomplished the work of 14 men; and tractors did the work of 72 men.

Now imagine someone then telling a Robert Theobald or some

other man who worried about technological change in 1870 that by 1970 farmers could feed nearly five times the U.S. population of 1870 with about one-fifth of the then existing farm population. What would he have made of such a forecast? Certainly he would ask where all the job opportunities were going to appear for the displaced persons?

There had to be a great exodus from the farm, and there was. We found jobs for farmers, the white male farmers anyway, in auto factories and steel mills, on the railroads and in the mines. Later we opened up opportunities for employment in engineering and technical work, sales, crafts, medicine, teaching, law, accounting, and business. These men were needed by the hundreds of thousands. We were a good deal less successful, however, in finding jobs for the farmers' wives and their daughters, and when we did, there were only a few occupations open to them.

In recent years we have had women and blacks as a reservoir since our youth reservoir of workers from the farms has almost been depleted. If—and it may be a big if—economic growth continues, we will need new contenders for the labor supply we need and they can only come from two groups, the women primarily, and the blacks, a much smaller group.

The blacks have entered the labor force from the farm and switching slowly into the lower scales of industrial jobs primarily, many into the durable goods sector of industry. Women are used in clerical and sales work and in health services and elementary and secondary teaching. If economic growth slows down or has to be curtailed simply because energy costs are going to skyrocket or if we aim at a national policy of some kind of zero growth in the economy, the problem of providing employment for blacks and women is going to be greatly exacerbated. In fact, women's relative wages over the past 50 years are less now than they were at the end of World War I.

Dr. Park offered a challenge to management in the last part of her paper, and it was offered in so low a key that it may not appear to say very much unless we pay careful attention to her meaning. She asks for "more flexible typing of professions and more imaginative scheduling of work [that] would profit men as well as women."[1] To be fair to women employees, we especially need to experiment with some less than full-time positions, and also to encourage women to assume and discharge as large a degree of responsibility as their abilities are capable. These are not minor or casual challenges. They will require, I believe, basic changes in society's attitudes and definitions of work. It means a reordering and a restructuring of business, industrial, and academic organizations. It may also require—and I think this is where the largest problem is apt to arise—that as a nation we are going to have to make a concerted effort to provide and create meaningful, monetarily rewarding activities for all adults, women as well as men. The fact that we have so many women carrying out routine tasks suggests that we yet do not see how we may accomplish that effort.

If we do make more room in the labor force for that large number of women who are ready, willing, and able to take positions at high levels, men may have to share their present jobs and positions. Career patterns, promotion ladders, methods of using talents, will have to be changed as well as hiring practices. I don't think that anyone at present knows how we are going to do it, or even how we should go about these problems. I doubt that we have really thought through the kind of complex problems that are going to arise when we try to respond to this challenge.

I am pessimistic that any of the answers are going to come easily, or that we'll even get very far. It may be that I am by nature a pessimist, but with any kind of turndown in the economy, I think it is probably going to be very close to insuperable to improve female opportunities.

There is one further problem facing us as women enter the labor force, and that is that black males are also seeking the same goals. There is already a good deal of competition between

---

[1] Rosemary Park, "Like Their Fathers Instead," Eli Ginzberg and Alice M. Yohalem, eds., *Corporate Lib: Women's Challenge to Management* (Baltimore: The Johns Hopkins University Press, 1973), p. 55.

them, and I think this is going to grow keener in the future, too. Data on the increase in net new jobs for blacks between 1963 and 1970 indicate a considerable increase in their employment opportunities. The largest number of new jobs occurred in the semiskilled occupations but 47 percent of the new jobs opened up in the professional technical area, outside of teaching and professional services, and in the nonsecretarial clerical area. Now in both of these fields women are also gaining jobs at a considerable rate, and they seem to me to be probably more open to women. Women may have already taken and may take in the future a fair number of jobs that otherwise might have gone to black males.

We have been exceedingly inventive in the past century in finding new jobs and occupations for white males, and what we've done since 1870 looks quite remarkable. We have helped them to move from agricultural work to blue-collar work and on to white-collar activities, rapidly increasing employment in government, nonprofit, and technical areas. It looks like a good record until we begin to consider all those in our population who have been left out. Then our imagination and our inventiveness do not seem to impressive.

Dr. Park has suggested that the greater part of our social and economic adjustments to industrialism have yet to be made. That is no small challenge to management and to the rest of the nation.

7

Sex Discrimination: Some Societal Constraints on Upward Mobility for Women Executives

Phyllis A. Wallace

This paper examines the role of women in executive positions in American industry. Many of the underlying issues of equal employment opportunity for women have been treated only superficially in the social science literature. Social and cultural factors, as well as economic and legal considerations, define the nature of the differential treatment of women in the labor market. Women who aspire to the more demanding elite or leadership positions encounter powerful obstacles to achievement of equality in earnings, job satisfaction, status, and power.

The increased labor force activity of well-educated and married women indicates that more women may perceive broadened occupational options. Consequently, there is a growing recognition of the importance of careers in the lifestyles of American women. Although the narrow focus of this review centers on an elite group—educated and talented women who may experience discrimination in employment—the efforts to improve their conditions of employment must be linked to the strategies for raising the economic status of large numbers of poor and minority women.

One could undertake a census of the elites in commerce, industry, government, and the professions by examining the rosters of officials listed in *Poor's Register of Directors and Executives, Who's Who in Finance and Industry*, the *Federal Register*, Dun and Bradstreet, professional directories, and the financial pages of *The New York Times*. A disproportionately small number of women—in terms of education, ability, experience, and recent substantial labor force participation—would be included within these prestigious ranks. A study of women in high level positions in business estimated that women executives (managers, officials, and proprietors earning $10,000 a year or more) numbered about 26,000 in 1960, or approximately 2 percent of the number of males.[1] A survey of women in business in 1969 by *Business Week* concluded that, with few exceptions, industry had as few top women executives then as it had had ten years earlier.

The growth in the number of salaried women managers and officials since 1960 has deviated substantially from what might have been expected based on the increase in the total female labor force relative to the total civilian labor force.[2] Only 3 percent of employed women in 1969 were classified as managers and only 4 percent in their category earned over $15,000.

The 1970 detailed census data will probably reveal broad occupational distributions that are similar to the 1960 benchmarks when women managers were concentrated in retail trade (mostly in middle management jobs), banks, and insurance companies (in lower level positions) and were heavily represented in what appear to be three low-wage occupations: postmasters, superintendants of buildings, and administrators in local government.[3]

Perhaps the clearest description of a subsample of women

[1] Garda W. Bowman et al., "Are Women Executives People?" *Harvard Business Review*, 1965, p. 23.

[2] Janice Neiper Hedges, "Women at Work: Women Workers and Manpower Demands in the 1970's," *Monthly Labor Review*, vol. 93, no. 6 (June 1970), p. 20.

[3] U.S. Department of Labor, Bureau of Labor Statistics, *Occupational Employment Statistics* (Washington, D.C.: Government Printing Office, 1966), pp. 18–19.

executives is that of those employed in the federal government. The U.S. Civil Service has attracted a large number of well-educated women who have moved into the executive ranks (grades GS-12 to GS-18). Because the salaries range from $14,000 to over $35,000, these employees—who include attorneys, social workers, accountants, chemists, editors, computer specialists, engineers, architects, and personnel managers—are more nearly representative of top level decisionmakers than is the broad managerial census category. The 16,205 women classified in these ranks in 1969 represented less than 3 percent of all women in white-collar government jobs and 5 percent of all federal executives. (See table 2.)

Table 2. U.S. Government Civilian Full-Time White-Collar Employment Executive Levels, 1969

GS Grade Level	Total Employment	Women	Percent
12	131,724	9,136	6.9
13	98,667	4,290	4.3
14	49,127	1,889	3.8
15	26,418	717	2.7
16	6,344	115	1.8
17	2,498	37	1.5
18	700	4	.6
Above 18	656	17	2.6
Totals and percent	316,134	16,205	5.1

SOURCE: U.S. Civil Service Commission, *Study of Employment of Women in the Federal Government* (Washington, D.C., 1969), p. 19.

Women have attained very few executive positions in trade unions and the military services. Of the 12,000 women officers in the armed services almost three-fourths are nurses. As late as 1968 only 35 women held either elective or appointive positions in national and international unions.[4] Women held 24 jobs (8 percent) of the 307 identified as exempt, unclassified, and

[4] Lucretia M. Dewey, "Women in Labor Unions," *Monthly Labor Review*, vol. 94, no. 2 (February 1971), pp. 42–48.

noncompetitive positions paying $17,500 or more in the New York City government.[5]

Almost two thousand executives, half of them women, were queried by the *Harvard Business Review* in a 1965 survey of attitudes about the role of women in high level positions in business. Half of the women executives in the survey were employed in companies with under 50 employees while 52 percent of the male executives were in companies with more than 1,000 employees. Some of the significant findings were:

1. Sixty-one percent of the men and 47 percent of the women believed that the business community would never wholly accept women executives.

2. Both men and women executives agreed that a woman had to be exceptional, indeed, overqualified, to succeed in management. (I call this the feminine version of the Ralph Bunche syndrome.)

3. Forty-one percent of the men indicated that they regarded the idea of women executives with some disfavor.

4. About a third of the respondents saw no opportunity for women in terms of equal access in labor unions, production jobs, and top management.[6]

To what extent will working women be allowed in the future to deviate from the cultural expectations of what is considered appropriate? Will strongly career-oriented women be relegated to a limited number of sexually segregated occupational categories? Does the sex-status of women as defined by the culture restrict their labor market participation to the lowest levels in the professional and managerial categories? A brief review of social and cultural factors merely emphasizes the gaps in our knowledge about the influence of sex roles on job behavior.

Social scientists offer a substantial literature documenting that the traditional roles of women are defined largely in terms of the sexual role. These have been institutionalized in the value system of the culture.

[5] City of New York, *Status of Women in New York City Government*, February 1971, p. 4.

[6] Bowman, "Are Women Executives People?" pp. 15, 19, 24, 28.

Cynthia F. Epstein has noted in her study of women's careers in the professions that "the typing of certain occupations as male or female has consequences for entry to them and performance within them by persons who possess the 'wrong sex.'" Women who seek entry to occupations defined as male are regarded as deviants and are subjected to social sanctions. "As a result, few women attempt to enter such fields and those who do often are blocked from the opportunity structure."[7] According to a recent report in *The New York Times*, an executive of General Motors admitted that women were generally excluded from General Motors recruiting for management posts.[8]

The saliency of the sex status of women in the employment situation has limited their entry to upper echelon positions, reduced opportunities for specialized training, and excluded them from consideration for promotion to the leadership cadres. The extent to which women are in the highest levels of employment depends heavily on their associations with peers and colleagues. These interactive processes (formal and informal) that often determine job success for all contenders for executive position rarely have been probed.

Social scientists have not dealt extensively with the issue of social sex role prescriptions in work groups made up of males and females. Margaret Mead's cross-cultural studies of sex differences in the aggressiveness/passivity dimensions of temperament indicate that the two sexes overlap to various degrees depending on the culture.[9] This suggests that job assignment should be based on strictly relevant, prior performance. A rival hypothesis has been advanced by Florence A. Ruderman. In her examination of some biological, cultural, and societal implications of sex differences she says that

[7] Cynthia F. Epstein, "Encountering the Male Establishment: Sex-Status Limits Women's Careers in the Professions," *American Journal of Sociology*, 75 (May 1970): 966–67.

[8] "Job Bias Against Women Earning Under Pressure," *New York Times*, January 31, 1971, p. 1.

[9] Roger Brown, "Sex and Temperament," in *Social Psychology* (New York: The Free Press, 1967), pp. 161–72. See also Margaret Mead, *Sexual Temperament* (New York: Morrow, 1935).

Sex differences which are manifest both anatomically and in reproduction are only, so to speak, the top of the iceberg; far more pervasive inner differences of mentality, temperament, drive, innovativeness are associated with these "external" sex differences. Sexuality is more basic and more diffuse than sex: it works through a complicated endocrinological system, a hormone structure, that makes male and female not simply the identical thing packaged differently—rather it makes them, in their nature, in their very being, unlike yet to some small but critical degree, essentially, qualitatively different.[10]

We do not know to what extent such differences may be related to the ability of women to perform effectively in executive positions.

Judith Laws in a provocative article has written that most observable characteristics of the female sex can be traced to social learning and shared meaning. The social behavior of girls indicates that girls do not reach out into the future—particularly toward the occupational world and higher education—in the way that boys do. The social expectations for girls represent reality-constraints. Professor Laws believes that social scientists have been proponents of a conservative doctrine with respect to women. It is status quo oriented with respect to relations between the sexes and illustrates the way social reinforcements are manipulated to insure conformity with norms.

The sexual identity is a distinct subsystem or subidentity within the overall structure of identity. Dr. Laws has hypothesized that

to the extent that a woman's sense of her sexual self is defined and anchored in terms of her self (rather than in another) she will make innovative role choices. If her sexuality is conceived as a part of the self rather than part of a role relationship, her perceived options will be less limited and less role constrained. Possible outcomes of such orientation might be greater work commitment (having a career instead of a job), later (or fewer) marriages, fewer children, and greater sexual activity—as fertility is controlled and sexuality

[10] Florence Rudeman, "Sex Differences: Biological, Cultural, Societal Implications," in Cynthia F. Epstein and W. J. Goode, eds., *The Other Half: Road to Women's Equality* (Englewood Cliffs, N. J.: Prentice-Hall, Inc., 1971), p. 49.

74

detached from the institution of marriage, it may be that other options become more salient for women at all stages of the life cycle.[11]

The higher the educational achievement of women, the more likely they are to respond to income and job incentives and to seek work.[12] The labor force participation rates for women with five years or more of college was 70.8 percent in 1968 as compared with 17.4 percent for women with less than five years of school.[13] Bowen and Finegan state that women with considerable formal education are likely to attach a higher value to the social interactions and sense of professional accomplishment that employment can offer than to the psychic rewards of staying home. A multiple regression analysis of selected variables indicates that when allowance is made for color, presence of children, age, other family income, and occupational status of the husband, a remarkably dependable association exists between education and labor force participation of married women.[14]

The educated women who comprise the potential resource pool for high level jobs in industry and government have experienced both wage and employment discrimination in a variety of jobs. We are using the International Labor Organization (ILO) definition of sex discrimination—"any distinction, exclusion, or preference made on the basis of sex which has the effect of multiplying or impairing equality of opportunity or treatment in employment or occupation." The employment discrimination against women is closely associated with their sex-status in society and the fact that many jobs are sexually segregated. Barbara Bergmann has recently developed a model of racial discrimination based on the Edgeworth idea of the "crowding effects."[15]

[11] Judith Long Laws, "Toward A Model of Female Identity," *Midway* (Summer 1970), pp. 39–75.

[12] Glen Cain, *Married Women in the Labor Force* (Chicago: University of Chicago Press, 1966); William Bowen and I. A. Finegan, *The Economics of Labor Force Participation* (Princeton: Princeton University Press, 1969).

[13] Juanita Kreps, *Sex in the Marketplace: American Women at Work* (Baltimore: The Johns Hopkins University Press, 1970), p. 24.

[14] Bowen and Finegan, *Labor Force Participation*, pp. 22, 115.

[15] Barbara R. Bergmann, "The Effect On White Incomes of Discrimination In Employment," *The Journal of Political Economy*, vol. 79, no. 2 (March/April 1971), pp. 294–313.

This earlier examination of equal pay for women and men argued that women received lower pay because they were crowded into a smaller number of occupations.[16]

Valerie Oppenheimer's analysis of the sex distribution of jobs shows

that different jobs get sex labels which persist through time, and that during the period 1900–1960, women workers were concentrated disproportionately in female occupations. For example, using the 1960 census data, eighty-one percent of all women workers were in occupations where more than a third of the workers were women. The observed percent was 2.1 times the expected percent (a random distribution based on overall representation of women in the labor force).[17]

The segregation of male and female workers into noncompeting labor markets, i.e., women workers in occupations which were 70 percent or more female, has usually meant payment of lower salaries to women. The U.S. Census Bureau reported for March 1970 that only 3 percent of women received money incomes of more than $10,000, compared with more than a quarter of the male income recipients.

Even where women may hold positions in predominantly male occupations they are allocated to the lower wage jobs. Employers perceive women as supplementary wage earners, intermittently in the labor force, and poor risks for on-the-job training. In 1968, the median income of year-round, full-time female managers was $5,635, only about 55 percent of the $10,340 median income of male managers. The Equal Pay Act of 1963, which amended the Fair Labor Standards Act, prohibits wage discrimination (equal work, same employer, same establishment) on the basis of sex. However, the exemptions in the Fair Labor Standards Act for executive, administrative, and professional

[16] F. Y. Edgeworth, "Equal Pay to Men and Women for Equal Work," *Economic Journal*, 32 (December 1922): 431–57.

[17] Valerie K. Oppenheimer, *The Female Labor Force in the United States: Demographic and Economic Factors Governing Its Growth and Changing Composition* (Berkeley: University of California Press, 1970), pp. 66, 69.

employees automatically applied in the amended act so that workers at these levels are not covered by its antidiscriminatory provisions. Nevertheless, the U.S. Equal Employment Opportunity Commission has held that women not protected against discrimination in pay by the Fair Labor Standards Act are protected by Section 703(h) of Title VII of the Civil Rights Act of 1964.

The gap in earnings between women and men reflects the fact both of the allocation of most women workers into low paying occupations and of some wage discrimination within the same occupations. In a recent study of male-female wage differentials in urban labor markets, Ronald L. Oaxaca attempts a quantitative assessment of the chronic earnings gap between male and female full-time, year-round workers. The discrimination coefficient (proportionate difference between the current average wage of women and the average wage that would prevail in the absence of discrimination) is estimated from wage regressions for each race-sex group. The discrimination effect accounts for 69 percent and 94 percent of the calculated male-female gross wage differentials for whites and blacks, respectively.[18]

Income differentials between male and female executives may be considerably larger than those apparent in the published statistics. Some fringe benefits, executive insurance, and investment in training may be restricted to males. Most of the stock option systems are designed by males to pay themselves more compensation at lower tax rates. Many companies pay membership fees for their officials to enjoy the privileges of exclusive executive clubs. Although business problems may be discussed in these places, women are rarely permitted entry to them. The American Management Association lists as one of the objectives of its management education program: "Gives you a chance to meet, influence, and learn from men who direct American Industry and Government." Few women executives are sponsored for these seminars.

[18] Ronald L. Oaxaca, "Male-Female Wage Differentials in Urban Labor Markets," Working Paper No. 23, Industrial Relations Section, Princeton University, mimeographed material (1971).

Working mothers must often assume heavy costs for child care. Until 1972, child care services had been barely covered under section 214 of the Internal Revenue Code. However, recent legislation permits families in which both spouses are employed and who file a joint income tax return to deduct up to $4,800 for child care depending on family size, if their gross income does not exceed $18,000. While this is a beneficial change for many working mothers, the imposition of an income ceiling prevents parents who are employed at high levels from availing themselves of its provisions. Many legislators are still unwilling to view payments for child care by working mothers as legitimate work-connected expenses since they are reluctant to accept the fact that the traditional division of labor between the sexes where child care services are provided by nonworking wives is no longer universally valid.

A broad child development proposal that extended day care services to children of all income groups was vetoed by the president in 1971. These services would have been offered to middle income families on an ability to pay basis.

Human capital development, especially investment in on-the-job training, is an economic consideration for women workers that has received little attention from the economists. Gary Becker's path-breaking work on human capital devoted less than three pages to rates of return to college educated white women.[19] Theodore Schultz noted at a conference on education, income, and human capital in 1968 that "in the work that has been done, the omission of human capital in females—should give us pause. But this troublesome omission, so it seems to me, can be taken on, and the rewards in terms of additional knowledge are likely to be large."[20] Most of the conceptual development, particularly on returns from education, has been modeled on males,

[19] Gary S. Becker, *Human Capital* (New York: Columbia University Press, 1964), pp. 100–102.

[20] T. W. Schultz, "The Reckoning of Education as Human Capital," in Lee Hansen, ed., *Education, Income, and Human Capital* (New York: Bureau of Economic Research, Columbia University Press, 1970), p. 306.

first college educated whites and later whites and blacks with other academic achievement.

Jacob Mincer recently presented a general formulation of the human capital approach to the analysis of personal income distribution. Costs and returns on investment in human capital are measured by earnings differentials. Individuals invest in education (training) in the expectation that their future income will be large enough to compensate for the cost (foregone earnings). Other factors such as ability and opportunity also have an impact on the distribution of earnings. Some of the differences between earnings distributions of males and females are explainable by the effects of labor supply behavior on human capital investment decisions.

Mincer has concluded that women are likely to invest less than men in the vocational aspects of education and particularly in on-the-job training because they expect to spend only a part of their adult lives in the labor force.[21] This item needs to be kept on future research agendas. For those women who may choose to invest heavily in advanced education, their participation in the labor force may more nearly match that of males.

On the legal front, the passage of Title VII of the Civil Rights Act of 1964 provided a new weapon in the fight for equal employment opportunity for women. Title VII prohibits employers, unions, and employment agencies from discriminating in hiring or firing; in wages, terms, conditions, or privileges of employment; in classifying, assigning, or promoting employees; in extending or assigning use of facilities; and in training, retraining and apprenticeship. This act guarantees equal employment for all persons regardless of their race, color, religion, sex, or national origin, and is administered by the U.S. Equal Employment Opportunity Commission (EEOC). In 1972, coverage of Title VII was extended to include employees of state and local governments and educational institutions and also of private employers of more than 15 persons.

---

[21] Jacob Mincer, "The Distribution of Labor Incomes: A Survey With Special Reference to the Human Capital Approach," *Journal of Economic Literature*, vol. 8, no. 1 (March 1970), pp. 1–26.

The EEOC was originally limited to interpretation of Title VII and investigation and conciliation of complaints alleging discrimination. Originally the burden of seeking enforcement through the federal courts rested mainly on the aggrieved individual. The commission referred to the U.S. attorney general selected cases involving a pattern or practice of discrimination and filed as a friend of the court in private actions. Under the 1972 amendment to Title VII, the commission may now bring civil suits against nongovernmental respondents. During 1969, women charging sex discrimination filed 3,572 complaints, or about 20 percent of the total.[22]

Executive Order 11246, as amended by Executive Order 11375 prohibiting discrimination in employment because of race, color, sex, or national origin by federal government contractors and subcontractors and on federally assisted construction contracts, is discussed fully in Michael Moskow's paper.

A large number of complaints have been filed on behalf of women faculty members charging more than 350 academic institutions with sex discrimination in hiring, promotion, and tenure. Few women hold high ranking teaching or administrative positions in American universities or colleges.[23] Although 14 percent of the 23,901 doctorates earned in 1968 were earned by women, this highly talented resource is underutilized by the institutions of higher education. A recent report from Yale compared the percentage of women teachers on the academic ladder of a major department with the percentage of women receiving the Ph.D. in that department within the preceding three years. Over half the doctorates (total of 53) had been received by women, but they held only 5 percent of the faculty positions.[24] Academic women are frequently not offered employment because they are

[22] Sonia P. Fuentes, "Federal Remedial Sanctions: Focus on Title VII," *Valparaiso University Law Review*, vol. 5, no. 2 (1971), pp. 374–96.

[23] U.S. Congress, House, Special Subcommittee on Education of the Committee on Education and Labor, *Discrimination Against Women: Hearings on Sec. 805 of H.R.16098*, 91st Cong. 2nd sess., June 1970, pts. 1, 2.

[24] "A Report to the President from the Committee on the Status of Professional Women at Yale," mimeographed material (May 1971).

80

married to academic men. The antinepotism rules of many colleges and universities deny equal employment opportunity to many women who wish to pursue careers on college faculties.

Many of the executives of the next ten to twenty years are completing advanced educational training today. I asked the deans of six graduate schools of business about the number of women students accepted and about the career patterns of recent women graduates. Because these views are instructive about the ways the school may help or hinder young women as they begin their professional careers, excerpts are quoted from two of the responses.

(1) It has only been within the last five years that the job market has begun to open up for women. Certainly the Civil Rights Act has helped in this direction, but the women's lobby has not been as strong as those of some other minority groups and consequently their progress has not been as marked.

However, there is a vast difference in the way they are received in the market today than was the case 10 years ago. In the earlier 1960's women were going into jobs which were traditionally women's jobs—retailing, research, personnel, etc. In the past five years this has changed drastically. True, women may have a harder time than men of equal ability but they are now entering such fields as labor relations, consulting, product management, account executive work, public accounting, corporate finance, marketing, banking, etc., which had previously been closed to them. The Wall Street area is even beginning to take on women graduates in what has, up to now, been a male stronghold. In a year such as this, however, when jobs are tight, it is my feeling that women have to look much harder than do their male counterparts.

(2) It is certainly true that in the past 15 years there have been more women admitted to this school than previously, though there have always been a few. It is my observation over the last six and a half years that these graduates follow career patterns similar to equally qualified males for the most part, though there have been several who have appeared to have followed the career patterns of their husbands and never really settled down to practicing at any length the trades for which they train.

I can close on the affirmative note of saying that I am certain that within the last three years, women have been more popular as hired in executive and sub-executive ranks. It has reached a point now where I feel they are definitely in demand in some companies much the same way and perhaps for some of the same reasons that black students are in demand.

A third school reported on the types of jobs held by recent graduates. The banking, securities, and computer industries employed most of the graduates. However, a few young women had started as marketing specialists in industries producing a variety of consumer goods. Perhaps women need to identify the growth industries and move into these new areas during the early stages of their development.

At the same time, strategies must be designed for dealing with the existing and familiar structures. It is generally conceded that today much of the employment discrimination against minorities results from institutionalized practices and policies of an informal nature. Similar institutionalized constraints handicap the movement of women into positions of power and prestige in society. We can identify many areas for future research and analysis. Some of the critical issues are:

1. To what extent will increased political participation by women enhance their social and economic position?

2. What do we know about decisionmaking at the household level that will be useful for a new approach to career-oriented families? In the past married women have tended to seek employment only after their husbands have decided on a location for their labor market activities. Will the tandem team approach with equally qualified partners mean that families will now locate where family income can be maximized? Thus, either partner could provide the primary source of income.

Equal employment opportunities for women executives are linked to the economic status of all working women, many of whom are heads of households who earn poverty wages. If well-educated women are advanced to positions commensurate with their qualifications, opportunities could be opened up for "working poor" women who now have limited options. I would like to urge social researchers to consider what might be some of the effects (benefits and costs), both on labor market processes and on social institutions, of expanding employment opportunities for women.

John Kenneth Galbraith has described "a new shift of power in the industrial enterprise—from capital to organized intelligence" and noted how this shift may be "reflected in the deployment of power in the society at large."[25] If the new emphasis will be on the team approach to decisionmaking and access to specialized information, the substantial number of young women presently being placed in entry level executive jobs may be permitted wider and more effective participation in the higher ranks of both the private and public sectors.

Basic economic models developed to explain racial discrimination have been assumed to apply equally to sex discrimination. Some modifications and alternative interpretations will be introduced as our perceptions of reality are clarified. Broader definitions of racial discrimination by federal administrative agencies and the courts have emphasized the consequences of discriminatory employment practices, not simply the motivation.[26] Such an approach is likely to have some spillover effect on investigations of sex discrimination.

The statement on "A Parallel to the Negro Problem" by Gunnar Myrdal in volume two of *An American Dilemma* outlines the similarities between the position of blacks and women: high social visibility, paternalistic treatment, conflict between achieved status and the ascribed status of inferior intellectual endowment, and rationalization of status.

Court decisions and the persuasive activities of several organizations have forced federal agencies to administer the racial and sex discrimination provisions of the law by use of similar criteria. Differences, if any, between discrimination in labor markets because of race and sex can be treated at the present time largely on intuitive grounds only. We know that women as a group are better educated than most minorities and accordingly have some competitive advantages. They are not outcasts in this

[25] John Kenneth Galbraith, *The New Industrial State* (New York: New American Library, 1968), p. 67.
[26] *Griggs* v. *Duke Power Co.*, 401 U.S. 424 (1971).

society and do not bear the stigmatization suffered by minorities. Nevertheless, thus far women have not challenged the business system through powerful coalitions such as those established by civil rights organizations.

One of the significant determinants of expanding employment opportunities for women at the executive level will be overall economic activity. In a soft labor market there may be aggressive competition between the educated elite of white and black men and women. One would expect the hierarchical ordering to be males, white and black, and females, white and black. However, a combination of more racial polarization, economic recession, and more militant demands by women may produce a far more disturbing outcome with educated and able white women and equally qualified black males fighting for token jobs in the executive suite.

8

The Sources of Inequality

Juanita Kreps

Inequality between the sexes is currently the source of so many inquiries that the researcher is being drowned in a mass of documentation. This complaint comes with ill grace, I realize, from one who has contributed to the statistical overload. Yet I do sense the need these papers express—the need to reach for perspective rather than for additional evidence of discrimination, to remind ourselves, once again, what it is we want to establish. It is said that Gertrude Stein, who was known to repeat herself occasionally, was still perplexed by it all when on her deathbed. With her remaining strength she inquired of her life-long friend, Alice B. Toklas, "Alice, what's the answer?" After some thought, came the reply, "Gertrude, I don't know." And after another pause, Gertrude persisted, "Then, Alice, what is the question?"

What are the questions we are now raising? Are they the ones we ought to pursue under the rubric of "Women's Challenge to Management"? One might, incidentally, question whether women are in fact offering a challenge to the business world; our present job status in industry would certainly not seem to lend strength to any such call to arms. In any case, if we are to examine the poor showing of women in the higher ranks of American industry, we clearly do not need further data showing that we have had only limited access to these positions. Rather, we need to ask and keep asking why the access is so limited, or why, at least, women perceive it to be so limited. And we ought to raise a second, quite different set of questions: To what extent are women eager to move into the executive ranks given the demands of that lifestyle? Do the family commitments women have traditionally made allow them the luxury of such ambition? Are there prior, intrafamily decisions to resolve before married women can compete effectively for the most consuming and demanding careers?

By everyone's agreement, business leadership has been an exclusively male calling and women have not been invited, tolerated, or even seriously considered. It helps but little to note in passing that just as women have been excluded, so, too, have practically all men; only the most aggressive, or talented, or lucky, or well born—sometimes all of these—have made it to the top. Still, I stress this set of credentials, not to excuse a discriminatory system, but to remind ourselves that freedom of access is a necessary but not a sufficient condition for executive leadership.

Why have men in industry been reluctant to admit women into their higher ranks? Have the performances of those few women who have tried to climb the ladder been poor? Is the threat of her dropping out for childbearing and childrearing the major deterrent to placing a young woman in an executive training program?

The first question is one that industry itself has to answer, and there may be too few cases to permit generalization. In assessing the value of women's contribution to business, however, we must be aware of two tendencies that confuse the issue: one, a woman may handle a particular job differently from the way a man would, and since a male judgment is the one that prevails, she may be thought ineffective when she is merely different; and two, it is sometimes hard for men to admire in women the very qualities they find important in successful men. Although failure to gain the admiration of one's superior may not be the only deterrent to promotion, it is surely a powerful one.

In a deeper context, there is the basic question of how willing men are to have their male world invaded by women, just as in the past, housewives have often protested having their husbands underfoot in the kitchen. Erik Erikson suggests that

no doubt there exists among men an honest sense of wishing to save at whatever cost a sexual polarity, a vital tension and an essential difference which they fear may be lost in too much sameness, equality, and equivalence, or at any rate in too much self-conscious talk.[1]

This fear of sameness may plague women, but, I suspect, not many career-oriented women. Nor is it the case still, as it used to be, that women tend to equate achievement with loss of femininity; hence "in achievement-oriented situations, women will worry not only about failure, but about success."[2] A woman's wish to achieve, one recent study found, conflicts with her wish to avoid success, for "if she fails, she is not living up to her own standards of performance; if she succeeds, she is not living up to societal expectations about the female role."[3] I discount this thesis for the kind of women who aspire to management.

There is also the matter of women's dropping out of their jobs at the childbearing age, a common complaint of businesses which are reluctant to hire female managers or interns, for example. Here, the picture is changing significantly. Observe the pattern of female labor force participation, by age, for the last several decades (figure 2). In 1940, young women left their jobs to have children, and older women, who had done so earlier in their own lives, did not return to the work force. By 1950, however, some of those women who had left to have babies a decade earlier were going back to paying jobs. By 1960, the second

---

[1] Erik H. Erikson, "Inner and Outer Space: Reflections on Womanhood," *Daedalus,* 93 (Spring 1964): 584.

[2] Joy D. Osofsky, "The Socialization and Education of American Women," in Ann F. Scott, *What is Happening to American Women* (Atlanta: Southern Newspaper Publishing Association Foundation, 1970), p. 37.

[3] Matina Horner, "Women's Motive to Avoid Success," *Psychology Today,* 62 (November 1969): 36–38.

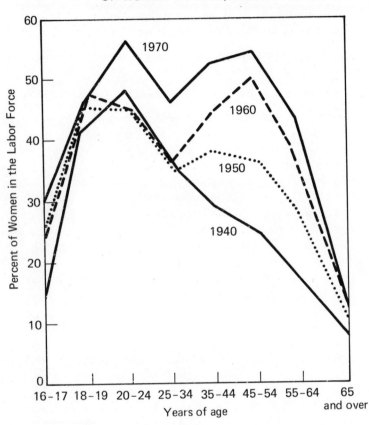

Figure 2. LABOR FORCE PARTICIPATION RATES OF WOMEN BY AGE, 1940–70

Source: *Monthly Labor Review* 93 (June, 1970), p. 11.

peak in the labor force participation of women, by age, was slightly higher than the first; the labor force activity rate was higher for older women than for young. Still, there was a deep valley between the two peak rates. But observe, then, the 1970 profile. Not only does it indicate much higher work activity at all ages than in previous years; there is also a much less marked drop in the rate at the age of marriage and childbearing.

An important question occurs. To what extent will the cohort of females now in high school and college leave the labor force during their twenties? If they find it desirable (and possible, with the help of child care arrangements) to stay on the job, industry will not need to discount so heavily their probability of acquiring experience and knowledge, and hence will no longer have this reason to deny these women access to higher level positions. It seems likely that the worklife patterns of this new cohort of women, particularly those who are college educated, will conform much more nearly to the pattern men's worklives have assumed. Such a change would have great significance for industry and the professions.

To what extent is industry's unwillingness to hire women for the better jobs due to the fact that women don't have wives? Has it been true, as often alleged, that the executive's wife was hired, along with her husband, and that she, too, was expected to add her efforts to the company team? If so, has industry not been able to get much more for an executive salary than it first appears, namely, the supportive services, the community activities, and the corporate image building of the man's wife? And while these roles are perfectly acceptable ones for wives, would they not be unacceptable for husbands? In short, does industry not reason, and quite correctly, that it gets more for an executive salary paid to a man whose wife's services also come in the package, than it would gain by hiring a woman?

I think the plight of executive wives has been exaggerated but an interesting, somewhat related question, has to do with high income wives, in general. Why is there an inverse relationship between husbands' incomes and wives' labor force participation (figure 3)? Are the demands of the husband's job, as his

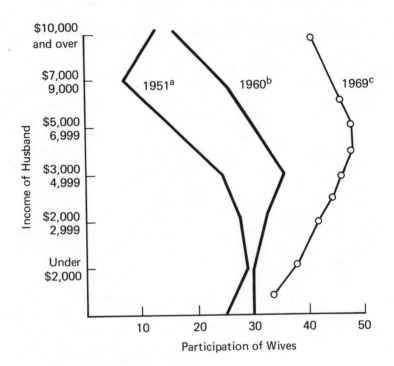

Figure 3. LABOR FORCE PARTICIPATION OF WIVES 1951, 1960, 1969 BY INCOME OF HUSBAND

a = All wives, aged 14 and over
b = Wives aged 20–24
c = All wives, aged 14 and over

Source: Bureau of Labor Statistics

Figure 4. LABOR FORCE PARTICIPATION RATES OF WOMEN, BY YEARS OF SCHOOL COMPLETED AND AGE, 1968 (18 YEARS AND OVER)

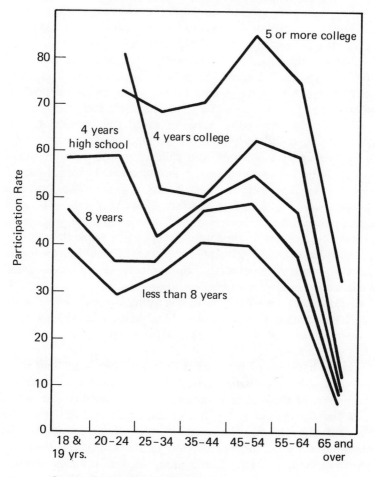

Source: Bureau of Labor Statistics

income rises, such that the wife has little opportunity to build her own career? Or do these women prefer not to work, once family income is sufficiently high? The puzzle is all the more interesting, since these men are likely to be married to college graduates, and female college graduates' labor force rates are higher than those of high school graduates (figure 4).

What are the signs of improvement? For a bit of history, I refer you to the National Manpower Council's study in 1957 which reveals something of how far we have come, and how far we have yet to go. We note that it was in September, 1957, that a New York City newspaper reporter asked four people at random: "What would happen if all working wives gave up their jobs tomorrow?" A secretary said children would get more attention, resulting in less delinquency; in any event, husbands earned enough to support their families. A singer, also female, said that the effect would be to give better jobs to working girls who really needed them, since "the majority of married women who go to business do so to earn money for luxuries like mink stoles. . . ." A man from Brooklyn thought that in time it would mean higher wages for men. A male post office employee said it would result in a better home life for husband, wife, and family.[4]

At that time, a similar poll in any American city would probably have yielded similar results. The question is whether public endorsement of women's campaigns in the 1970s indicates any significant change in attitude. It is clear that large numbers of women have joined the protest, and it is significant that these are increasingly the young women, many of them still in school. The impact of these younger women on the woman worker a few years from now will surely be an important one. I personally fear that these younger members of the protest movement are somewhat naive in their perception of the opposition they will face from some quarters. Commenting on the attitudes revealed in the earlier interviews, Erwin Canham noted the problems ahead: "Look at the misconceptions; look at the jealousy toward

[4] From Esther Lloyd-Jones, "Education for Reentry into the Labor Force," in National Manpower Council, *Work in the Lives of Married Women* (New York: Columbia University Press, 1958), pp. 27–40.

married women on the part of the interviewed females . . . ; the jealousy, possessiveness, and prejudice on the part of men."[5]

At the family level, the constraints on women's upward movement in the ranks of both industry and the professions are being eased by reduced family size. The current societal goal of zero population growth confirms youth's view that they should have, at most, two children, in contrast to the grand design of the women of my generation, most of whom were determined to have six. Fortunately, some of us lost sight of the goal about half way there. But certain family constraints remain much the same. It is still true that the wife has little option as to the location of her job, and this immobility is surely a prime factor in her limited career advancement. Some of the most exciting jobs in industry are those that demand geographical mobility, not just within this country, but to other nations as well. These avenues are simply not options for married women. Or, at least, business assumes that they are not, and rarely asks a woman whether she *can* move.

In time, a wife's job may become sufficiently important to the family to allow that job to take precedence over her husband's. But for now, the wife fits her career into a framework dominated by her husband's work and the needs of her children. These constraints are the fundamental ones on the supply side; they limit the time and attention she can devote to her career, the degree to which she can take advantage of career opportunities, and in the final analysis, her career aspirations. It is not surprising that women do not press harder for entry to the executive suite; would a woman not need to be single to have any realistic hopes of success? If this is true and women are becoming more ambitious, we may see a growth in spinsterhood. And in that case, will men accept single women as "normal?"

Whether or not they are so accepted, it seems likely that in the future more women will remain single, or seek divorces; careers will inevitably absorb the interests of many competent women who no longer need the financial support of husbands,

[5] "Womanpower in Today's World," in ibid., p. 14.

and who are not particularly interested in having children. There is some evidence of growing social acceptance of unmarried females, and contraceptive methods make it unnecessary for these women to forego sexual relationships.

Among married women, who will nevertheless continue to include most women, it seems unlikely that marriage and child-rearing will again assume the central role it assumed for women formerly. The working wife and mother is not a new development; on the contrary, nonworking wives are a product of modern technology and affluence. What we are concerned with here is, of course, not whether women will work, but what their work will be—at what level, and with what rewards, demands, and satisfactions. And what we are asking, on the *supply* side, is whether we want to reconsider male-female career priorities and intrafamily responsibilities in such a way as to accommodate greater career flexibility for both sexes.

What we are asking on the labor *demand* side is: What are the pressure points we can lean on, to challenge industry's traditionally antifemale bias with respect to the higher level jobs? It should be noted that in other sectors of the economy the same problem exists. The academic world, too, has "his" and "her" jobs, with females concentrated heavily in the lower ranks in all universities. So, too, has government; both academia and the government ought to be setting standards, not lowering them.

What are the things we ought to do? In directing our thoughts to specifics, I should like to stress two things we ought *not* to do. The first concerns research. We are looking for points of attack not just a basis for complaint—we know things are very bad. If we earn 59 (and not 58) percent of what men earn, we will scarcely notice the difference. My first curb, then, would be on narrowly based statistical inquiries; they are a waste of scarce resources. Phyllis Wallace's references to lifetime earnings is, of course, a different, and very important thrust. In teaching human capital investments, I am unable to compute the returns for women and am forced to talk only of men.

I would also banish from the media those writers who criticize women's seeming lack of professional ambition—criticism which, under close examination, usually emerges as praise. To writers, the preoccupation of the female with love and marriage is fully accepted. It is only when she displays "the old-style careerist's scorching ambition and hostility toward men"[6] that she has to explain herself. It is true, further, that many men and women resist taking women's new career interests seriously. No dinner party is now complete without a few derisive comments on women's ambitions to be stevedores or lumberjacks. I realize that members of both sexes are apprehensive, men perhaps more than women: "Where dominant identities depend on being dominant, it is hard to grant equality to the dominated."[7]

In a positive vein, what can be said? What, in addition to the recommendation that women go into the courts with cases of discrimination?

First, the notion of second careers for men as well as for career women seems quite appealing, since it would open up some good jobs at high levels, and condition us to think of new worklife patterns for both sexes.

Second, it is obvious we have to present some goals to top management: some numbers of women to be hired, or promoted. This will have to be done by personal contact, on a company by company basis, although in the universities we are getting a large assist from HEW.

Third, it is obvious that recruitment—much of it done on our campuses—has got to be rigged in such a way as to promote the selection of women. If I were running a placement office I would not allow inequitable interviewing arrangements, and I would keep very careful records on who hires women and for what jobs.

Fourth, I think we should never underestimate the power of women's threats. If you have ever faced an angry group of women, you know that it makes one very nervous. How can we get groups of women to act in such ways as to make corporations

---

[6] Morton Hunt, *Her Infinite Variety* (New York: Harper & Row, 1962), p. 262.

[7] Erikson, "Inner and Outer Space," p. 585. "And finally, where one feels exposed, threatened, or cornered, it is difficult to be judicious."

nervous? I should like us to use this method sparingly; but it can be used.

I am optimistic on the long-range future—if we can keep the pressure on—because I see so clearly how many light years ahead my own daughters are, beyond where I was when in college. For the immediate future, I am considerably less optimistic because the state of the economy is so uncertain. We pay a price for slowing down the economy. It is much easier to solve most problems of absorbing new groups into occupations and jobs on the upswing of business activity. And this we don't now have. Universities, under orders (more or less) to hire more women, can do so only if they are hiring somebody—and they are adding very few people.

I asked for no more research. But I would leave, in passing, a couple of questions that are general, framework sorts of questions—those that set the parameters of the problem. One of these has to do with the amount of work each of us is to do—can it be changed so more people work at good jobs, but each for fewer hours?

The other question has to do with the timing of work through the life cycle. It may be that we will make substantial progress in absorbing women into all levels of jobs only when we agree on a retiming of work for both sexes. For example, we now witness retirement as a relatively new life stage. Could we imagine periods of reeducation or sabbaticals, or just plain vacations—thereby spreading one's work differently? This would extend options, not only for new careers, but also for coming in and going out of jobs in accord with individual preferences—and would be infinitely preferable to taking our leisure in the form of unemployment or prevention of women from working.

I am not sure we all agree, quite yet, on how much flexibility and "sameness" we want. But I am sure that relatively few women will reach management's top levels under the constraints imposed by current expectations: those of the society, the family, and the woman herself.

9

Family Life of the Successful Woman

William Goode

I have commented elsewhere that women will be the last group in our society to be freed. I see no reason as yet to change that opinion. The pious hopes and optimistic public relations announcements of corporate steps toward sex equality in hiring and promotion exhibit a depressing similarity to those in the areas of race or to those in pollution control. With reference to the latter, I sometimes suspect there is a high correlation between the self-praising public relations brochures and annual reports about their good deeds and their persistent violation of good ecological principles. That is, the worst offenders spend the most on proclaiming their good conduct.

Even if my dismal view is not entirely correct, I do not believe that male managers can be easily persuaded that they should make room for even able women. We should not underestimate either their cunning or their staying power, and least of all, their motivation. They are convinced of their own special superiority, and of women's inferiority, and will yield only grudgingly and slowly. Where they do yield, they will try to put women in the kinds of jobs that pay less, have less influence, and offer less opportunity for advancement—in short, jobs fit for women.

97

That managers will be exceedingly clever in this strategy can be inferred from one great generalization about the sexual division of labor in all societies. Although a few tasks are allocated only to men in all societies, such as quarrying, big game hunting, and so on, and a few only to women, whatever tasks are defined by the society as dramatic, challenging, or fun are almost always socially viewed as men's work. That is, I think, the only evidence I know of the *general* superiority of men over women.

Male resistance can take many forms, because the problem itself is so complex. Consequently, if one negative argument is refuted, our male tradition supplies us with many more to deny opportunity to women. Little progress will be made, in any event, as long as we argue about whether men are superior to women. The question is entirely irrelevant, just as it is in race. Any hiring or promotion policy that is based on such a belief is not simply erroneous—although there is much evidence that it is—but simply beside the point. The question is rather if that particular person is the best we can get, not whether the group to which he or she belongs is superior. It is the individual's performance that counts; we are not after all hiring his or her group.

Similarly, and much more closely linked with my inquiry, the oft repeated rationalization of male managers that women should not be hired because their duty is to children, home, and husbands is not only irrelevant but also an impertinence and a subterfuge. For we do not ask our potential male recruits whether they are going to marry and have children, or neglect their wives and children. Indeed, I would suppose that in a highly productive and competitive firm, as in a university department of high achievement, we rather suppose and even hope our candidates *will* neglect those outside distractions somewhat and give their best talents to the enterprise. Surely we should adopt the same policy toward women.

I have strong doubts that corporations will suddenly hire entirely on the basis of merit and potential. After all, they have done very well in the past without following so drastic a policy. Nevertheless, I shall assume, as a purely speculative stance, that they will perceive a near identity between goodness and wisdom, and that over the next two decades we shall observe a sharp increase in the utilization of womanpower in higher managerial jobs. What then will be the consequences for the family? Can we expect catastrophe, or new harmony?

I might argue, if I did not feel I would be considered facetious, that since management is inherently and organically a woman's job, females should experience no great change, shock, or dislocation in running a corporation and a family simultaneously. If our stereotypes of women are correct, the skills and behavior they acquire in becoming a woman are exactly those of good managers: they are trained in human relations, not test tubes and machinery; in insight; in the organization and maintenance of a social unit, the family; in command not through arbitrary orders, but through persuasion and participation; in taking care of subordinates and serving their needs so that they will produce better. If they can become good homemakers, surely they could become excellent managers.

To explore the possible impact of a woman's being a manager on her family life requires more, however, than an assertion that the two tasks may be similar. In a different kind of social or economic position, people change, and we need to ask, how are they likely to change? Since, however, we cannot know the future, I must make my predictions on the basis of the dynamics and processes we now understand, the facts about family relations that we now know.[1]

Of course, if we were to confine our examination to the mass media, we would already know the answers. In that never-never land, high level women executives have no difficulty at all in managing a complex family life as well as the problems of entrepreneurship or administration. Both the women's glamour magazines and the mass circulation magazines publish from time to time a report on one or more of the few hundred top level

---

[1] I have learned that a recent Ph.D. dissertation concerns itself with women executives, but I have not been able to obtain it: Margaret Hennig, "Career Development for Women Executives" (Ph.D. diss., Harvard School of Business Administration, 1971).

female managers in the country. Since these magazines have for many decades attempted to reassure the American woman that family life is a great experience, but simultaneously like to describe success stories, they are forced now and then to show how women executives make it. However, they are also required by their own ideological needs to locate only those women who have made it but have also succeeded in efficiently or harmoniously running a household as well. It does not take much cynicism to note that the cases are presented precisely because they are exceptions: specifically, they are newsworthy because we are surprised that it can be done at all.

I bring up such cheerful portraits, not simply to remind you that we cannot draw any powerful generalizations from such descriptions, but to bring to the center one of the two most powerful variables with which we must analyze the future of family life among women managers, that is to say, the budgeting of time and energy. Specifically, we are surprised by such portraits because we cannot imagine how we ourselves could manage so far-flung a dual empire, and many of us finish reading those reports with a general feeling of exhaustion.

Before looking at the problem of time and energy, let me note that the other major variable is that of women's independence. The striking, relevant, phenomenon in industrialization is not that women were put to work. After all, women work in all societies, and in most of them do much of the dirty, drab, and tedious work. It would therefore not be surprising that they were put to work in factories at the very earliest stages of industrialization.

What was different, however, was that for the first time women were hired and promoted as individuals rather than as women attached to and subordinated to some man. Although it would take much too long to explicate the chain of causation, I am convinced that this is one of the most important variables in the slow change of status among women over the past century and a half. It is especially important with respect to entrepreneurship. Although women have been heads of companies in the past, they have typically got there because of some family connection, very often as widows or heiresses. What is now proposed is much more radical: we are now proposing that women should be put in the topmost positions of large corporations, as men are, whether or not they have inherited large blocks of stock, or the company itself, or because they are married to someone who has a high political or corporate position. Without any question, this will increase their independence substantially, and we must consider the impact of that change upon family life.

Let us, in any event, consider the problem of time and energy as a general matter, before we embark upon some of the specific predictions that I shall be willing to make about family life among top level women managers in the future. That is to say, we must begin with the obvious, because the obvious often structures or shapes many solutions that we can imagine for the decades to come.

I should like to phrase the problem in the form of a general rule: that is, the successful manager, male or female, needs a wife. What shall we be able to do about it in the future? Perhaps I can phrase the matter more sharply, by asking you to consider what would their family life be, if the two male presidents of General Motors and IT&T were married to one another? It can also be phrased in the mild complaint to be found in a thoughtful article about equality in middle class families: ". . . behind the working wife with young children, there stands a tired husband."[2]

It is important that we face up to this challenge to the imagination, for we are trying to guess what might be the family life of women if they tackle the difficult problems of managing corporations. Inevitably, if they do, some will be married to other top level managers, since one of the major regularities in marriage is *homogamy*—people of the same class, education, race, ethnic group, religion and so on, usually marry each other.

We already know a good bit about the time budgets of top managers, and we cannot suppose, without anticipating major

[2] S. M. Miller, "The Making of a Confused Middle-Class Husband," *Social Policy*, 2 (July/August 1971): 37.

changes in the society, that the work patterns of women managers will be any different. Even if we allow for a pardonable exaggeration—whose aim is partly to inform others how big a burden they carry, partly a plea so that others do not make additional demands upon them—high level managers, professionals, and research scientists all work very long hours indeed. They are more likely than perhaps any other segment of the work force to work seven days a week, and to take work at home in the evening as a matter of routine, if they in fact return home before it is time to go to sleep. Moreover, as we all know from personal experience, such skewed time budgets are important because they are an index of where the person's energies, talents, and attention are focused. It is not merely that the manager spends long hours at his tasks; he is likely to be thinking about those tasks most of the time, no matter where he is.

The other side of the coin is equally evident from our knowledge of the time budgets of women. Contrary to popular opinion, the amount of time that women spend in homemaker tasks has not diminished over the half century. It is true not merely in those countries where the blessings of American civilization in the form of rapidly obsolescing home equipment have spread to a large part of the population. It is also true for the United States.

The basic dynamic in this fact is one that Marx remarked on over a century ago when he posed the question as to whether labor-saving had indeed saved any working man any labor. We do not need to accept his labor surplus theory of value to understand that he perceived an important fact about the machine, that it does not so much cut down the amount of work that men do; rather, it increases production. This has been true in the home as well. Women no longer draw and carry water. They do not set up great cast iron kettles in the back yard where wood fires boil the weekly washing. Most do not scrub floors on their knees any more, and women can now buy their frozen chickens in the supermarket, instead of raising them, wringing their necks, and plucking and cleaning them by themselves.

On the other hand, for every such task that seems to be simplified or diminished, the housewife has taken over other tasks or has instead simply raised the standards for cleanliness, while help from other women has diminished. Our houses and all our clothing must be cleaner than a century ago. Servants and kinsmen do not help us in our clothes washing. In short, the modern homemaker does in fact have a wide range of appliances to use, but she also turns out more production in a given 10- to 14-hour day.

Underlying this fact is the basic dynamic of all machines and indeed all bureaucracies. They are brilliant and fast in carrying out very specific, limited tasks, but they are also very stupid in tasks that require integration, in handling crises, in nonspecialized tasks, or in tasks that require human relations. None of our appliances, for example, will pick up a diaper or straighten a living room after a cocktail party. Moreover, no machine will socialize our children for us or pay attention to our wives or husbands.

With reference to children, as Alice Rossi pointed out a few years ago, we are perhaps the first civilization in the history of the world that has decided that parents must transform the socializing of children into a 24-hour-a-day job, and has given this job to women. In former civilizations, children began various kinds of work at early ages. They lived among adults and parents did not spend much time wondering about how to entertain them. It was supposed that children owed a great deal to their parents, rather than the reverse. Although many may agree with this modern concentration of attention upon children, it is at least obvious that if the family of the future is to continue this pattern, we have posed a nearly insoluble question for families of women managers—no matter who is to bear the burden of socializing the children, husbands or wives.

However, that last statement poses a further challenge to our imagination, in this attempt to make predictions about the future. For if we examine it closely, it really states that if nothing is to be changed in the family system itself, it might be better if women who perform at the highest levels had no families at all. Or, perhaps we might turn it about and say that men who ought to perform at the highest levels ought not to give such hostages to fortune as families and children—and indeed, perhaps that was a more common pattern in past centuries, except for political leaders. Nevertheless, we do suppose that the social structure is changing, if at a less than satisfactory rate.

Moreover, we know that most of the people who will become top managers in the near future, whether men or women, will have been socialized in the present era, so that their attitudes will be incongruous with the needs of the future. During the next two decades, if our optimism is at all justified, some new men and women will appear who will be able to solve some of the family problems that now plague us. Consequently, we must imagine in our speculations a kind of moving belt on which people in all stages of transition may be found. We also recognize that as a larger number of women become top level managers, and as a larger percentage of the top social stratum takes on different attitudes toward sex equality, the daily life patterns of adults will respond to those changes and they will behave differently. Thus, there is a continuing alteration, and even those who are changing will also face a new and changing situation throughout their lives. That is to say, we cannot assume a time present and contrast it with a time future. We must also imagine an interim period in which all these gradations are present and in which a steadily emerging and a perhaps erratically emerging set of changed attitudes will be encountered.

Let me begin by making a prediction that relates to a mixture of stereotype and reality and that is important for the phase of courtship before marriage. I make the prediction that women managers will in the future be perceived as much sexier and more womanly than at present. At the present time, men who actually serve under a woman manager are less likely to harbor a negative stereotype than are men who have never worked for a woman manager. Yet we are all familiar with the two general pictures that men, especially, and perhaps most women as well, hold about women managers. They are tough, cold, bitchy, and castrating women.

A second stereotype is that women managers are slightly frivolous but cunning; they use their feminine wiles and tricks to get their way. I shall spend no time in trying to refute this stereotype, but I shall point out to you that here is no corresponding stereotype about men. As many social analysts have pointed out, men are people; women are not. We give special characteristics to women as a class, but not to men. Without being able to weigh what core of truth there may lie in this stereotype, as in so many stereotypes, we can at least note that any subgroup that faces substantial discrimination, negative labeling, insults, and rejection is likely to exhibit a number of disapproved sociopsychological traits in its effort to break the barriers. This can be observed in every area of ethnic relations. It would be surprising indeed if the many kinds of discrimination that women meet in their effort to rise in the corporate hierarchy did not have any effect upon their behavior, self-regard, attitudes, and even perhaps personality structure.

Men are permitted several different kinds of styles, each of which gives them some bits of respect, along with some deprecation. Thus, for example, some men are permitted the role of "mad genius." These men are stimulating and produce a vast number of ideas, not all of them very sensible, but some of them excellent. They are permitted to be careless about details, and even about their dress. They lose a few social points for not being conformists, but they gain admiration for their problemsolving abilities. As another example, men, and even some executives, especially if they hold large blocks of stock in the corporation, are permitted the role of roisterer and man about town. They have an extravagant style, enjoy interesting love relationships, and indulge themselves in many pleasures—but at the same time carry out their executive tasks with some panache. I am sure that everyone can think of men with other styles of work not quite in accord with the conformist image that most people have of corporation executives.

Note however that none of these styles is permitted to women. If a woman is a roisterer and a woman about town, she loses points and gains none. She is not therefore thought to be more womanly. If a woman is careless about details and sloppy in her dress, she loses points without being permitted to adopt a mantle of mad genius. In short, women are permitted a much narrower range of social roles to play and thus a much narrower range within which they can express their normal personalities, needs, motivations, and personal styles.

However, to the extent that corporations begin to utilize the imaginations and skills of womanpower, they will have erased many of the barriers that at least played a part in generating some of the behavior that men especially now view as un-womanly or offensive. Phrasing the matter in a positive way, success doubtless brings with it many burdens, and not all of us react well to success, but it is safe to say that most of us are easier to live with when we are successful than if we are failures or if we have been blocked by discrimination. Those who have been both rich and poor know that rich is better. Managers often have to make difficult decisions in which they decide the fate of subordinates, but almost certainly those who have experienced success can handle the situation with greater warmth and sup-port than those who feel threatened, who are viewed as deviant, or who are faced with prejudice.

I've also said that success is sexy. And I believe this will in the future apply to women as well as to men. I will not here exam-ine the dynamics of this relationship with respect to men, but few who have had the opportunity of observing successful men would deny the general fact. I do not even view the dynamic as grounded in a cynical calculation on the part of women. In fact women do find men who are successful more attractive, and not simply because they can buy mink coats or purchase weekend trips to Puerto Rico.

I am however extending the dynamic to women, and I be-lieve that it applies to some extent even now. It will apply more in the future, as we stop thinking of women executives as being deviant, odd, and unwomanly, and as they permit themselves to be freer in their tasks and work styles. Even now, although I would not go so far as to claim that most high achievement men find high achievement women attractive, I believe that more of them are able to enjoy their competence, the range of their con-versation, their animal magnetism, than can men who are less successful. The latter are too commonly worried about their own masculinity, about impressing the woman, about their need to be dominant. To the extent that we can simply accept a woman executive as another human being of high accomplishment, we shall be able to respond to her human qualities and enjoy her mastery of the job challenges with which she has been faced.

This also means that it will be easier in the future for women executives to be married. They will be worth more on the marriage market. To the extent that they have experienced a more egalitarian atmosphere, they will not need to hold tight against the impact of emotional involvements as much as in the past and perhaps will not even have the need, so common among women, of finding a man whom they judge to be their superior. Since, in fact, that number of men is statistically small in any period, women often have not been able to find men who could tolerate their achievement or whom they judged to be superior, and so they viewed their choice as being one between marriage and career. I believe that this will not be so necessary in the future. More men will want to marry them and they will be freer emotionally to commit themselves to a man.

I believe, however, that one element in the women's liberation movement will have some impact on what kind of marriage relationship will be viewed as tolerable. I think it is at least possible that more men and women in the immediate future will live together without marriage for some time because they do not wish to enter the kinds of legal entanglements that marriage in all states now requires. In the longer term future there may be a movement toward more marriages that are based upon an explicit contract. That is to say, increasingly some small part of the professional and administrative strata in our society will try to work out a set of formal contractual relations that spell out as precisely as possible what each mate's obligations are; how the two of them shall operate a joint household; and under what conditions and with what penalties they will be permitted to leave it.

I cannot predict that in the future married women managers will have fewer children than at present, because without question their fertility at the present time is low. In general I predict and fervently hope that the birth rate of the United States will continue to fall, and I believe that our future social health requires not merely zero population growth but a reduction in population. I believe that some part of the upper occupational strata will respond to this need and that top women managers will be among them, but I would predict that the increased percentage of such women who marry in the future will balance off the possibly slight decline in fertility among those who do have families.

I have already offered a relatively gloomy prediction as to marital harmony in the future in this occupational group, if far more of them are given the opportunities their talents merit and no basic changes in the family structure occur. I base this upon the two powerful variables of time and energy budgets, on the one hand, and resources for independence, on the other. The first problem, as women especially know, is not solved by either housekeepers or the increased willingness of men to help their wives out at many junctures, such as by babysitting, dishwashing, or occasionally cleaning up, delivering the children to their various after school activities, or even preparing outdoor barbecues for guests. These chores are not to be belittled, but they are relatively small contributions compared to the overriding burden of directing a household. I would characterize the nature of this job as containing hundreds of items that have relatively low importance but high urgency.

Women can accomplish much less than men in their chosen areas of creativity, not because they have no free hours— homemaking is an intermittent task, punctuated by many relatively free time periods—but because there is no uninterruptible time. There are no periods in which the woman can know with certainty that she can turn her energies totally to a creative task. She is also socialized to respond to these household urgencies. Therefore, it is much more difficult for a woman to get any creative work done at home than it is for a man. Most men, even those who have accepted with deep conviction the philosophy of equality in the home between men and women, have been also socialized simply not to respond to many household crises. They are able to ignore them. Often, they do not see them at all;

if they do see them they feel no inner impulse to do very much about them; and if they are pushed to do something about them, they are irritated and incompetent.

Correspondingly, even if there is a satisfactory housekeeper, as there is likely to be if there are two substantial incomes in the family, the woman is expected to assume the major burden of seeing that all the activities go forward smoothly and efficiently. Indeed, in the portraits and vignettes in the mass media, to which I made reference early in this paper, the women executives are described as efficiently running their homes, but in no instance have I encountered any description of a male executive who efficiently ran his household, thus freeing his wife to do high level creative work. The contrast is striking and challenges our imagination to think of better solutions.

Indeed, so much have we failed in this challenge that one frequently now encounters young women who assert that they will simply not marry at all. This is very different from the choice between career and marriage that once faced the determined woman fifty years ago. These young women like men and are willing to live with them. They do not, however, wish to start a household and utterly refuse to begin directing the household so that some man can achieve better. During this interim period, although the number of such women will certainly not be large, I think that a goodly number of men will find themselves in a position that was not common in past generations. They will be trying to persuade women that they should settle down and take part in the joys of home life, just as women once pleaded with the attractive bachelor to settle down to domesticity.

Certainly, if men continue to pay as little attention to their marriages and homes as they do now, family life among women executives of the future will be rancorous, unsatisfying, and unstable. Abler women, whatever their public façade, have certainly accepted the main philosophy of women's liberation, and they will not weaken in that conviction. I think it is a safe generalization about revolutions that once the natives have seen the possibility of a successful rebellion, they never return to being happy contented natives again.

On the positive side, however, is a considerable amount of

evidence—still incomplete and unsatisfactory, it must be granted —to the effect that although there is somewhat more conflict in families where women are working, there is also likely to be much more satisfaction as well. Moreover, if we look at the narrower cell of working women who like their work, quitting the job and "going back to the home" is simply not a viable alternative. Men who push in that direction are headed for marital catastrophe. The problem is rather, given the increased desire of able women to take on challenging jobs, how much men are willing to give in order to achieve a relatively new mode of marriage in which both of them can be fulfilled. The woman who enjoys her work is easier to live with, and she will be impossible to live with if she is not permitted to work. Consequently, my basic question is not so much whether women can rise to the new challenge, as whether men can do so?

I do not believe that I can offer a successful solution, but before making an attempt I must introduce the second major negative element, the variable of independence. It is a truism in role and exchange theory that people who have high resources can be and are more independent in their decisions. People who enjoy more alternatives, whether in marriage and love, or in jobs, can afford to be and are more independent. People who have the grand resource of an exciting job are likely to be less upset at the defection of a friend, of a potential customer, or even of a wife; and this will hold as well for women managers. They will be much less vulnerable to the economic threat of divorce. They will have their own network of friendships.

There are many reasons why the general rate of divorce is higher at the lower social strata, but certainly one factor is the much greater potential losses of women in the upper social strata as a consequence of divorce.[3] The discrepancy between their potential income and that of their husband's is much greater than in the lower economic strata; males in those upper strata have the potential alternative of choosing among much younger

[3] I have analyzed the factors in some detail in my book, *Women in Divorce* (New York: The Free Press, 1965).

and more attractive women; the social and friendship networks are determined primarily by relations among men, not women. These wives thus feel, and correctly, that they may be left behind in case of a divorce. By contrast, the successful woman manager has far greater resources: her income is high; her social and friendship network is to a great extent her own; she possesses many advantages to offset in part the disadvantage of years. Even this disadvantage may diminish to some extent in the future if we really come to accept egalitarianism, because at the present time we have managed to define as attractive and interesting the kinds of lines in a man's face that would be viewed as haggard in a woman's. Perhaps that too might change.

In any event, it takes no great sociological wisdom to predict that with an increased basis for independence, an increased element of instability is built into the home life of the future. The philosophy of many at the present time would hold that instability is not a problem, except for those who hang on to the myths and hang-ups of the past. In the new fluid future, they say, we will enjoy what relationships come along and float as easily to the next as we floated into the last one, with little bitterness or hurt and only a delighted anticipation about the future.

I do not wish to criticize this as an ideology but I am convinced that for only short periods in our lives can we enjoy such instability. To the extent that the other person is emotionally meaningful to us, we care greatly whether that person goes or stays. It is never enough to know that somewhere in the future we may encounter another person who will please us. All of us have some deep insecurities about our own worth, and we would like not to wonder each day when we return home whether the other person has now decided that it is time to go.

People in the future, like people in the past, have a deep need for emotional continuity. To the extent that instability is rife and both husband and wife make it quite clear in advance that the relationship depends only on the daily fluctuation of emotional attachment, both will invest far less in that relationship, be committed to it far less, and will more quickly end it if there are difficulties or problems. It then becomes a pleasant and easy

111

companionship for the moment, but it is hardly likely to generate deep loyalty or to yield deep satisfaction. I want to emphasize here that I am stating what I believe to be fair guesses about the psychological dimensions of affection; I am not making moral statements about how people ought to behave.

If much of this analysis is correct, we once more face the challenge to imagine how we can, in the face of impossible time budgets and great independence of both partners, create any foundation for a stable and fulfilling relationship. A romantic falling in love may initiate the marriage; after that, what will keep it going? I believe that the question is worthy of attention, even though it must be confessed in advance that we have not solved the problem of engineering happy marriages for women and men who are *not* at the top levels of management.

It may seem paradoxical, but I foresee far less effect on children than on the husband-wife relationship, and much of that effect—except for the instability of divorce—I believe may be useful for children. It will certainly be psychologically more healthful for girls to be reared in an atmosphere in which it is taken for granted that they will use what talents they have. If girls are not pushed into the world of dolls and carriages, housekeeping, and pretty clothes and instead are allowed to express their bent for chemistry, truck driving, entrepreneurship, and the arts, that can be only productive for them as well as the society.

I believe that such a set of norms and behaviors will also be healthful for boys as well. For though our present system does push them to high endeavors, it also deflects them from talents and skills that they might otherwise find delight in exploring. For example some boys might well become excellent homemakers and not waste their energies in the occupational world. Doubtless in the past, and even at the present time, thousands of talented boys have been turned away from dancing, choreography, many other arts, and teaching because in some circles these are viewed as sissy. We have created in males a high degree of anxiety about their own masculinity and this has created in turn some viciously spiral problems in their sexual relations, their adjustment with women, and for that matter, in their professional lives.

In the world of politics and business, many men have made bad judgments because they felt their masculine honor was at stake. Many men find it difficult to give or even to receive warmth from others, men or women, because they feel it is unmanly to give way to their own emotions. We ought, as a consequence, not to be deeply concerned if, in a household in which a top woman manager helps to create an atmosphere of equality, some part of her sons' masculine pride is diminished. We could well do with less of it in the modern world.

However, that statement is of course a value judgment. I am expressing both a prediction and my approval of what will take place. But my deeper conviction is that, although parents perceive children as extremely recalcitrant, and as having very little of the plasticity that some social scientists have imputed to them, I believe that children are able to adjust successfully to a much wider range of parental practices than we have believed. I believe that children can even thrive in an atmosphere of somewhat more neglect than they experience at the present time, especially in the upper middle strata. Parents would also be better parents, better able to give love when it is needed, if they did not feel so anxious about what terrible consequences they may be creating by their socialization patterns. However, it is much more likely that we shall move toward somewhat more salutary neglect if husbands take a fair share of the burden of childrearing. Women will not feel the same need to justify their intense concentration on the home if they have an outside job that is both fascinating and demanding. Since under that type of system, both husband and wife would be much more open emotionally to each other, I believe that children would still obtain sufficient loving.

I do not believe that the analysis of a problem, or the prediction of difficulties, carries with it a moral obligation to offer solutions. Each one to his own métier. I have, in any event, predicted some good consequences for family life that may arise when far more women assume top positions in management. Nevertheless, I wish to comment on at least some aspects of solutions that have been offered, including in particular the possibility of Consciousness III coming to play a large role in our society and therefore in the family lives of women and men executives.

I will not analyze the theoretical shortcomings of a particular book. In that connection, my colleague Amitai Etzioni has remarked that Charles Reich's book *The Greening of America* is the *Love Story* of social science, and we need not be detained long on that particular version of the future. We must, however, take seriously the possibility that we are at least at a potential watershed in the history of our country and indeed of Western civilization, and it is at least possible that, for the first time in the history of the world, a major civilization at the height of its powers is making a reassessment of its goals and quality of life and will move in a different and creative direction. No prior civilization has ever done this and I think it is unlikely that we shall do so, but we must at least consider this possibility with reference to the narrow focus of this discussion.

In that new world whether or not it is coming, we would not rejoice if the automobile industry sells 7,000,000 vehicles a year; we would be outraged. We would not plan for quick obsolescence. We would subtract from the gross national product the pollution, destruction and general costs that our production brings with it and would strive to increase satisfaction rather than the number of products. We would decide that war is unprofitable, as we have decided that colonies are unprofitable, and we would spend almost nothing on the war industry, since it does not enhance the quality of living and, as many propaganda buttons have reminded us, it is bad for children. We would have a zero population growth and would recognize that we are the custodians of natural resources, having no right to destroy them. We would not give honor to people who win battles, but we would give honor to people who achieve greatly in friendship, love, and the creation of warmth and friendship. We would invest much of our social science research in learning how to create the conditions for personal fulfillment, democracy and participation, and even beauty.

I do not wish to argue that this Eden is possible, but without question a substantial minority of our coming leaders now believe in some part of it, and they will not be totally converted by their entrance into the life of the corporation. Indeed, as most of you know, their impact on even Wall Street law firms and major corporations is already visible, and not alone in the development of new clothing styles. We do not need, then, to suppose that a major reorientation of our civilization will occur, in order to confront the fact that an increasing number of people in the future will believe some part of this philosophy and try to act upon it.

One proposed solution for family life is some form of the commune. I believe that a very tiny percentage of people will continue to try that experiment, though I believe that all communes will have an extremely high rate of turnover and will not furnish a viable solution for the problems I have outlined. Nevertheless, such social units do solve to some extent the problem of the care of children, since it is much easier to socialize and to provide for children in a group. It is indeed the fragility of the husband-wife combination that makes this problem loom so large at the present time. If either dies or leaves, the number of adults has been reduced by half. In urban life, very young children cannot be allowed out without some supervision and, if both husband and wife are intensely involved in a job, they simply cannot be around much of the time. A commune does offer a partial solution for that problem.

Women's liberation has also argued for a widespread day care program, which at the present time is not emerging with any great speed. It too would offer a partial solution for the child care problem, and of course such centers may be mainly available in the future for those with higher incomes, so that the families of women managers can take advantage of them. On the other hand, such centers are not predicated on any major change in the society.

One element in this vision of the future is that people will not be so compulsively work driven and will divert far more of their energies and talents to other human beings rather than continuing to be tools and instruments for the purpose of production.

One proposal in support of that philosophic ideal is that men and women might develop far more flexible plans for their lives. For example, we might inaugurate a plan whereby either husband or wife might work only part-time for rather lengthy periods in their lives, or might alternate at work—men staying home for, say, six months and then turning the homemaking job over to their wives. Or, each might work part-time, spending some part of each day at home and some part of the day at work.

If we respond to still another element in this vision, we would not insist that children spend the most active part of their day in schools from the time they are five or six years of age until they are in their early twenties but permit a much more widespread integration of work and education, as was typical throughout most of our history. To that degree, the child care problem would be reduced, as would the problem of integrating the schedules of husbands and wives.

By making each home an independent factory which takes care of its own washing, ironing, cooking, shopping, cleaning, etc., we have in effect burdened the wife—and in the future we must expect to burden the husband—with a vast array of recurring tasks. To that end, some have offered the solution of large-scale housing units, not in this case true communes, in which there would be communal preparation of meals, services of various kinds, cleaning, and the like. I confess that I personally can adjust to most of this, but I cannot face the problem of institutional cooking. I deplore the creation of a future society which will on the one hand lay great stress upon beauty and pleasure but look down upon an investment in culinary delights. Nevertheless some part of this is at least possible.

Moreover, we can propose a slightly different alternative based upon the prediction that a great number of things are possible if one has a high income. If there are many top level women managers, and most of them are married to men who also have a high income, it should be possible then for a number of such families to band together and create small communities within the same general area—they need not be in the same village—in which the range of services necessary to run households is provided by an organization for that purpose. The house-wife or househusband would not have to have a long list of telephone numbers of carpenters, electricians, handymen, garden-ers, cleaners, etc., and would not have to spend time in negotiating with each one. Instead, they could make their wishes known to the central organization which would take care of it from that point on. That this is not an impossible solution can be seen from the fact that this is precisely what we do in the corpora-tion itself. Dozens of small-scale tasks are simply delegated. One of the advantages of that delegation is that the husbands and wives could then spend far more time with one another and in far less conflict about who must do which tedious task of the household. If that were done, it is quite possible that we might build into these marriages a slight increase of stability, for any wise husband or wife would not quickly leave so comfortable an arrangement.

It should also be kept in mind that we do not have to work out a single solution for all of the men and women of the future. Each of these solutions that I have noted may serve the needs of some couples and not others. It is, in any event, almost cer-tain that if we do not change the present family patterns, there is no chance at all of achieving even a modicum of equality in the occupational world. If we do move toward equality, we shall create additional problems. However, it is possible that as we continue to contemplate the necessary changes in the future, we shall see not only the possibility that they will yield more fulfill-ing lives for men and women, but we shall also be able to apply our creativity to effective solutions for the new difficulties that arise. In any event, as I noted earlier, I see no way of returning to the past. Whatever the difficulties of the future are, we must go forward to meet them and to overcome them. We are no longer the same people we once were, and it is no longer even within us to recreate the past as a form of adjustment. We must rather rejoice that we are getting rid of some of the diffi-culties of the past and look forward with some anticipation to a chance of fulfilling ourselves by confronting the problems of the future.

10

Family Life in Transition

Elizabeth Janeway

Let me begin by recording my concurrence in a great deal of what Professor Goode had to say. My remarks will be in the nature of extensions and addenda for the most part, though a few caveats come to mind.

In order that my discussion may be seen in context, I should perhaps say that my own view of family change is that it has never ceased and never will. Specifically, I believe that the breakup of the nuclear family began more than a hundred and fifty years ago with the rising importance of the factory system. If, as Philippe Ariés suggests, the appearance of the family as we know it dates from not much earlier than the seventeenth century, we can see that the reign of the parents-and-children home, occupied only as a place of residence, was brief indeed. Its importance is clearly as an ideal, a mythic symbol of affection, understanding, and privacy. It is a powerful symbol, but it needs more than emotional drive to make it a reality.

It was a reality at a time when the nuclear family operated as an economic unit. The family farm, along with cottage industry, supplied an economic base for the operating nuclear family. The factory system, predicated on employing individuals as labor producing robots, began the breakdown of this kind of family operation, which has now been completed. Today, what most people live in, or with, is the *less*-than-nuclear family. Working fathers are absent from home during most of the day, the children are schooled outside it, and practically all women who work for money must go outside to earn their living. The economic function of the family has disappeared, and so have many of its social uses. In the words of Kenneth Keniston, it "has become specialized in the related tasks of managing feelings and bringing up children."[1] In my opinion, it does neither of these things as well as it might largely because it has been cut off from close participation in the larger public processes of the economic and political world. I am, consequently, not greatly disturbed by the idea of change in family lifestyles. In fact, it may well be change for the better.

Professor Goode is surely right in believing that the effort of men to keep women "in their place" will not end easily. Most men believe quite sincerely that women belong there and are happiest there. The most substantial force working against this archaic idea is that, within the last few years, *women* have finally begun to oppose it in a concerted way. Their own acceptance of supporting roles and of gaining rewards vicariously through the emotional appreciation of others will not disappear overnight, but the effects of women's liberation consciousness raising (an idea that has found its time) are beginning to be apparent. The greatest barrier to women's advance in the public world of action has been their acquiescence in the idea that they don't belong out there. This inhibition is now weakening more and more.

On women as managers, Professor Goode paints an amiable picture of the role of housewife as manager, but he overlooks an important managerial factor where women's past experience has left them deficient. They have not regularly functioned as conscious and overt decisionmakers, even within the family. Decisionmaking is difficult for anyone in a complicated world, and

[1] Kenneth Keniston, *The Uncommitted: Alienated Youth in American Society* (New York: Harcourt, Brace & World, Inc., 1960), p. 294.

119

the family has not been a center of important social activity for a long time. Action decisions are especially difficult for those who have had little practice in facing them and whose role contra-indicates such behavior. I might say here that I think Dr. Goode rather overestimates the real demands of housekeeping before and after the extremely busy years when a young mother must cope with children and house and emergencies with no support. During that period she may, as he suggests, have to work a ten- to fourteen-hour day in the house. It is seldom more than a matter of choice, however, for a woman to continue on such a schedule once her children are in school.

We might note here that the disappearance of domestic servants has had a profound effect—and one too little noticed publicly—on family life and the ability of women to undertake outside work. The effect of this social change is usually swept under the rug by current morality: the idea that traditional domestic jobs are oppressive and immoral. I shall not dispute this idea. Maybe these jobs are. However a possible substitute might be trained, skilled employees, working moderate hours under specified conditions, plus centers for more than custodial care of children. I raise this point because the sweeping away in the last fifty years of almost all regular and permanent assistance to young mothers is so seldom considered seriously. To speak from experience: I have always been able to employ adequate domestic staff, and I have *never* been unable to pursue my own career. One of my daughters-in-law has no children, minimum help, and a full-time demanding executive position. My other daughter-in-law has two children under four, minimum help, and just within the past few months has been able to take on a part-time job. All of us worked before marriage and, as far as capabilities for employment are concerned, I would say there is nothing to choose between us. The differences in how much we can undertake lie in the support we can muster for outside activity.

As Dr. Goode remarks, the job of socializing children has been made more demanding in our present-day civilization than in most others, and it has been handed to women—a situation which is, as he says, unique. The fact that work of economic value can no longer be done at home puts women in an even greater bind. If they must earn (and most women who work do so because they have to earn), they have no choice but to leave the home to get employment. And they have, today, *no social support* which will help them by offering them alternative care for young children. Children of working mothers are often looked after by hit-or-miss, patched-up, inadequate methods; and their worried mothers know it. Industry, I note, is beginning to become aware of this and some public spirited companies are setting up day care centers for children of their employees. It is to be hoped that many more will do so, and that tax write-offs for such projects will be established. I believe that companies will gain access to an employment pool of reliable and mature workers by such methods.

It is clear from Dr. Goode's paper that he is aware of the need for such support for working women *below* the managerial level, but not convinced of its pertinence to the problem of putting women into the upper echelons of business, government, or educational institutions. As I see it, a major hindrance to the steady rise within business of capable women is discontinuity of employment. Such discontinuity is lessening, but it is still a large factor in the *thinking* of management. Consequently, it seems to me, the need for social or company support of lower level women is vital to upper level women because it permits those who will *become* managers to keep their places on the escalator while they are in their younger years. In addition, it validates the assumption that capable women will work, and will be able to work, at their chosen professions for all of their lives.

And it is just this question which Dr. Goode raises with such sympathy and insight when he advocates the *individual* approach to the promotion of women. Let me join in heartily on this crucial point. Management should make it a rule always to offer an employee promotion, even if such promotion demands a geographical move, a time schedule, or any other prerequisite which might seem to be difficult for a married woman to comply with. If the woman is capable of making management decisions, she should be capable of making one about her own life.

Dr. Goode's comments on the greater variety of lifestyles open to man managers than to women are indeed amusing. Women who deviate from the image of a womanly woman "lose points," he says, and this is no doubt true. It is well to point out, however, that this is much less true in certain areas of life where women have been acclimated for a fairly long time. In the arts, for example, women have been allowed for decades to live unconventional lives without losing any points. I doubt if this is because singers, writers, actresses, painters and so on are thought of any more as "Bohemians." That appellation is pretty old-fashioned. It is more likely that they have gained the freedom to live their own lives because their achievements have been judged for so long without relationship to sex. It may be hoped that as women become more usual and accepted in management, their eccentricities will become less objectionable.

When we come to the effect on children of having working mothers, we come round again to the question of our own norms. I have spoken of the disappearance of regular domestic help with no socially acceptable substitute offered. This has been paralleled by the weakening of community and neighborhood ties and the mobility which scatters families away from their roots, so that the old extended-family pattern of help in child care is decreased in incidence. In my opinion there can be no solution to these difficulties *within the family*. Certainly it will profit every member of the family (good nature and willingness being present) for fathers to interact with their children more. But this is far from enough. As Dr. Goode says, communes are only a partial (and in most cases a very marginal) solution; but, some kind of "clumping," of which communes are an example, is needed by children as well as parents. Children today suffer from too limited a number of adult models to copy, and, at the same time, from too restricted and sometimes too intense a relationship with those who are close to them. What we need, I repeat, is *social* support for the family which will broaden its connections to the outside world and provide a multiplicity of channels of communication toward children, so that their socialization by parents is supplemented; these channels will work in other directions, too, allowing the talents and energies of women and children to break the bonds of too-narrow homes. Particularly valuable is Dr. Goode's suggestion that work and education be reintegrated, as they once were.

In conclusion, I think management will solve its immediate problem of finding women managers by imaginative search within its own ranks. My experience with small and semismall industry indicates that very capable women can be found when management knows them personally, in ways that are possible within smallish business units. Few women, as yet, are likely to volunteer for upper rank jobs in industry, government, or to some extent, education. Moving into management is a much more daring step for women to take than management men understand. The life of a role breaker makes constant psychological demands. Proper behavior is not a settled, accepted thing, but has to be improvised, thus calling for recurrent decisions of all levels of seriousness. The sheer impact of facing and evaluating novel situations can be wearing. The possibilities for inappropriate action increase, and inappropriate action invites laughter and produces shame. Even when behavior and action are appropriate to what needs to be done, they may be misunderstood by the others involved in the situation. The life of a woman volunteer for a management job is especially precarious because she is vulnerable to all manner of sabotage from men—or thinks she is. And I wouldn't be sure she is wrong.

It seems to me that managements which really want to get capable women in their upper ranks are clever enough to do it if the will is there. Why not have a competition to work out game plans which will put competitive men managers in a position to profit from the success of women trained within their departments so that the men are competing with each other for points which can be gained only by successful women? The rewards could be long-term and cumulative. One of the lacunae of present experience is that few men in management have worked *as equals* with women. So why not arrange such operational togetherness by, for example, putting men and women on committees to plan company projects together for vacation employment of young people? (No doubt this would need union support, but is that impossible?) Why not sponsor day care centers that aren't called that but something like "Childhood Enrichment Environments," to be administered by churches or educational institutions jointly with industry, and at the same time start training women *and* men to work in them?

Frequent comment has been made to the effect that one career problem for women was that all successful managers needed wives, and women weren't allowed to have them. I had always been amused and appreciative of this observation but suddenly I wasn't. It occurred to me that what women—and men —need to be successful managers is not a wife apiece, but a *staff*. At the moment, I want an efficient filing clerk and a fifth of a good secretary. Look at it the other way round, which is the important way: too much of wives' time is spent on staff duties instead of on wiving. This is a justified source of grievance. Most household duties are really staff duties. There is no reason on earth why I always pack my husband's suitcase, only habit. Fortunately, we have arrived at an arrangement in which he takes everything to be packed out of the closet and I put it in the bag—an acceptable labor saving device for us both. But this is staff work; a valet could do it all.

Let me suggest that some brilliant young management group will cut through the soggy myths of the past, of "how it is always done," and will tap an inexhaustible source of energy and imagination by finding out how to use women, their energy, drive, stamina, and imagination. At the moment, most of management is sucking its thumb and wondering how to avoid doing this. Well, as Julia Child would say, "Bon appetit!" But wouldn't management really rather have a good meal? That is, wouldn't it prefer a larger, richer talent pool for employment at high levels than it is now drawing upon?

11

Government in the Lead

Michael H. Moskow

Discrimination in employment by federal government contractors and subcontractors because of race, color, sex, or national origin was prohibited by Executive Order 11246, as amended by Executive Order 11375. Under this order, the Office of Federal Contract Compliance was established within the Department of Labor to administer its provisions and to coordinate the activities of all federal contracting agencies. My discussion will cover the activities of the Office of Federal Contract Compliance, and I will generalize a bit about some of the parallels and contrasts between problems of minorities and problems of women.

The United States government purchases about $70 billion worth of goods and services each year from firms that employ an estimated one-third of the labor force, including all of the country's large employers. These are the contractors covered by the compliance program. For example, if we look at the banking industry, we find that the program covers all banks insured by the Federal Deposit Insurance Corporation, all banks that sell and redeem savings bonds, and all banks that have federal funds on deposit—and that virtually exhausts the banks in the United States.

The compliance program is very important because it gives the federal government immediate and powerful leverage to discourage discrimination in employment. There are certain procedures that have been established to use this leverage—such as conciliation, show-cause hearings, and consultations—but ultimately the federal government has the power to refuse to do business with someone. It can cancel, terminate, or suspend existing contracts, or it can bar a contractor from receiving future government contracts. These are very powerful economic weapons to discourage employers from discrimination and to encourage them to take affirmative action to employ minorities and women.

The Office of Federal Contract Compliance is a unique organization in the federal government. The government could have organized all persons involved in federal contract compliance into one agency which would have dealt with all contractors and subcontractors. Instead, it was thought that more effective results would be obtained if compliance officers were part of the contracting agencies themselves, so that they would work as a part of the regular contracting process. The only exception is in the case of universities with federal contracts whose compliance is supervised by the Department of Health, Education and Welfare, regardless of the contracting agency.

The bulk of the compliance staff, then, is in the contracting agencies. The Office of Federal Contract Compliance is responsible for coordination of contracting agency activity, for issuing rules and regulations, and for monitoring the contracting agencies and the compliance officers. From our point of view, this division of responsibility makes much more sense than having one central agency, since it permits the question of equal employment opportunity to be considered as part of the entire contracting process.

Here are some figures that give an idea of the magnitude and growth of this program. In fiscal 1969, the Office of Federal Contract Compliance had only 26 people on its staff, and a budget of $600,000. This fiscal year the staff has risen to 119 people and the budget is $2,500,000. In the contracting agencies, in fiscal year 1970, there were 643 people and a budget of $7,000,000 and this fiscal year there will probably be over 1,500 people and a budget of $21,000,000.

Order Number 4 was issued by the Department of Labor to delineate the criteria to be used by federal contractors in developing plans of affirmative action to increase employment opportunities for minorities. Affirmative action requires the government contractor to go beyond refraining from employment discrimination. The contractor is required, as part of the contracting process, to analyze his work force and to determine whether there are deficiencies in the utilization of minorities. If there are deficiencies, the contractor then must formulate written corrective measures, including goals, timetables, and a plan of action for their elimination. These written corrective measures are required to be established for each job classification. Together, they comprise the contractor's affirmative action plan.

Generally, a "job classification" is a job for which the wages, functions, and opportunities are the same. If several jobs are related in these respects, they can be combined into a single job classification for which one set of goals and timetables is sufficient. If they are not so related, there must be separate goals.

The contractor's affirmative action plan is kept on file and it is subject to periodic review by the compliance agencies. The Office of Federal Contract Compliance has developed an analysis form, called form A, which the contractors use to expedite their analysis of their work force. This will also provide a data base for use in measuring overall progress or lack of progress.

In 1970, certain guidelines were issued to cover sex discrimination. These guidelines were a stopgap measure to make the commitment of the federal government to equal employment opportunity apparent, while buying time in which to develop a detailed affirmative action program for the employment of women.

According to the guidelines, employers with women employees have to provide them with various facilities, such as locker rooms and rest rooms, and cannot refuse to hire women on the basis of the nonavailability of these facilities. A second guideline stipulates that employers cannot refuse to hire women because of restrictions existing in the so-called state protective laws. The federal government regards all these laws as preempted. Third, employers must make certain accommodations for female employees, such as allowing a reasonable period of leave for childbearing.

A revised version of Order Number 4 was issued in December 1971, presenting criteria for the utilization of female workers, since the original order had applied only to minorities. In effect, the revision extended the mandate for affirmative action to women. This revision was developed after consultation with employers, women's groups, compliance agencies, minority groups, etc., and it tailored the principles and procedures dealing with the underutilization of minorities to the problems of the underutilization of women.

Contractors are required to revise any existing written affirmative action programs to include changes embodied in the order. They are also required to communicate to employees and to prospective employees the existence of their affirmative action programs and to make available the essential elements of their programs to allow the employees and prospective employees to avail themselves of the benefits.

When a contractor undertakes an analysis of his work force, Order Number 4 requires that he take the following criteria into consideration in determining female utilization.

First, he must consider the size of the female unemployment force in the labor area surrounding the facility. Second, he must look at the percentage of the female work force as compared to the total work force in the immediate labor market area. Third, he must consider the general availability of women having requisite skills in the immediate labor area. Fourth, he must ascertain the availability of women having requisite skills in an area in which the contractor could reasonably recruit, outside of his immediate labor market area.

Next, he should inquire into the availability of women seeking employment in his labor or recruitment area. He must also note the availability of promotable *and* transferable female employees within his own organization. He should have some idea of the anticipated expansion, contraction, and turnover of the work force—its growth or lack of growth. Finally, the existence of training institutions capable of training persons to develop the requisite skills and the degree of training which the contractor is reasonably able to undertake as a means of making all job classes available to women are important considerations. The contractor then must arrive at goals and timetables for the employment of women, based on these criteria.

The criteria for women are similar to those for minorities, modified to meet the particular problems attendant to sex discrimination. Where deficiencies are found, the contractor is required to establish separate goals and timetables for women and separate goals and timetables for minorities. The order provides that if it comes to the attention of the director of the Office of Federal Contract Compliance, or the compliance agencies, that there is a substantial disparity in the participation of different minority groups, then separate goals and timetables can be required for each of those minority groups, such as for Spanish-Americans, for Indians, or for Orientals. If substantial disparities are found in the employment of men and women of a particular minority group, separate goals and timetables can be required for males and females of those groups. We plan to monitor these figures for minority and sex subgroups very closely to insure that problem subgroups are separately treated.

In terms of implementation, a search for evidence of sex discrimination is included as part of the general compliance review that is made of a contractor. The person making the review looks at the distribution of the work force by sex as well as by race, religion, and national origin.

The general compliance review is automatically conducted for any supply contractor with a contract of more than a million dollars before the contract is awarded. Other contractors are chosen for a general compliance review based on apparent underutilization of minorities or women revealed in part by the Equal Employment Opportunity Commission annual compliance reports. Specific individual complaints are referred to the EEOC for investigation.

To give some idea of the number of general compliance reviews, in fiscal 1969 there were approximately 8,000 of these reviews. In this fiscal year we estimate that about 44,000 general compliance reviews will be completed. Next year we expect that number to increase to about 60,000. In our potential universe there are probably 250,000 contractors.

My own view is that Revised Order Number 4 represents a very significant change in public policy. No longer are we simply going on record against sex discrimination, although that was certainly a necessary preliminary step. Now we are requiring tangible evidence that meaningful steps are being taken to improve the employment prospects of women. This order goes beyond merely prohibiting discrimination against women to stimulating the recruitment of women. The great strength of the order is in the use of the federal government's compliance apparatus to put some teeth into the effort.

It will no longer be sufficient for a government contractor merely to refrain from overt acts of discrimination against women. Instead, he must present evidence that he has made a viable plan for finding and employing women who are potentially qualified for his work force.

There are parallels and contrasts between public policy regarding discrimination against minorities and against women. Let us look at some of the parallels. First, the obvious similarity is that the provisions of the Executive Order and of Order Number 4 now apply both to minorities and to females. Another parallel is that mere enforcement of equal pay for equal work will not suffice to bring about equality of opportunity for either group. Women, like blacks and other minorities, suffer not only from low wage rates relative to others in the same job but also from being denied entry into prestigious, well-paid, and challenging occupations. Both groups suffer from unequal opportunities for advancement and promotion, which means that an activist policy requiring affirmative action is a necessity.

Let me mention two contrasts between the situations of women and minorities. In the past, the status and income available to a married woman has depended primarily on the success of her husband, and she has found it in her interest to support his cause, although this may conflict with her own career interests. I do not think that minorities find it in their interest to support the interests of whites in that way.

The primacy of the husband's career interests operates as a constraint on the equal opportunity movement, as many married women are content either to play the traditional role of the housewife or to engage in labor market activity from a disadvantaged position. However, both male and female attitudes toward the appropriate role of married women are changing rapidly; over time this voluntary barrier to equal opportunity may be lifted.

Another difference between women and minorities is that there is really no approximation among the latter of the particular situation resulting from childbearing. Clearly, here is another area where attitudes are changing on the part of both men and women. Nevertheless, childbearing often continues to involve a long interruption in the work experience of women. By long interruption, I do not mean a month or two months leave, but five years or more, until the children are in school.

When the female is off the job for five years, her male counterpart is on the job. He is learning and building up human capital, as the economists would say. When she returns after a five-year break in her employment, the woman will clearly be at a disadvantage. She is not going to have the same skills or the capital that he will have built up in that five year period.

This has an important policy implication. If that type of break in the career of a female is to be eliminated or greatly reduced, is the development of improved day care facilities on a massive scale a prerequisite? We have already seen some steps in this direction. An attempt was made in the last session of Congress to pass a child development bill which would subsidize the child care expenses of poor and near-poor women. Another start in this direction is the proposed Family Assistance Plan. Here, child care would be provided specifically to facilitate the employment of welfare mothers in an attempt to help them leave the welfare rolls. It is a job-oriented type of child care service.

Both the extent and the type of child care to be provided for poor women are still under debate at this time. I mention it because I think it is one policy that attempts to ease the entry of women into the work force on a large scale.

Hopefully, the emphasis on affirmative action will facilitate the achievement of equal employment opportunity for women. In the battle against job discrimination, the compliance program of the federal government should be an effective complement to existing legislation. The compliance weapon enables us to reach about one-third of the U.S. labor force. Although it cannot have an immediate impact on the entire labor force, we believe that this effort will have a substantial impact and will significantly advance the equal opportunity movement.

12

The Larger Stakes

Charles De Carlo

It seems clear that work has a different meaning in the United States now than it had 200 years ago, when there was a shortage of labor. Then, the family was the basic work force; each member from the age of five or six had a role to play. Everybody had to work for life to have meaning, if not dignity. With the development of technology, labor was divided into specialized functions, and the centrality of work within the family unit began to break down.

Technological change meant more than steam machines. The real revolution was the growth of new corporate institutions that became independent with a life of their own. They were, as Justice Marshall defined them, entities of the establishment clothed in the guise of men. In fact their scope exceeded that of the individual for they were able to ensure the continuance of their existence.

The rationalization of the world through technology and corporate enterprise is seen as a major achievement of American business and government. It had negative effects, however, on the role of women. No longer were women important elements of the work force. When work became formalized, complex, and specialized, women found few roles in the labor market. They were confined to occupations that developed out of what had been women's work 200 years ago—nursing, childrearing, teaching, aiding businessmen as secretaries, and working around the house. These results were compatible with a sexual double standard. Males had most of the power and most of the privileges including the best jobs.

The effects of technology on our society have been far reaching. If one works around the house all day, sooner or later Parkinson's Law takes effect, and the work expands to fill the available time. This damages the credibility of the household as a meaningful work unit. In the same way, much of what is done in both the factory and the office is meaningless in human terms. This is not to deny that work performs a social function by enabling people to interact. But work itself—the specifics of work —is frequently meaningless.

I began to test this idea during 12 years in industry. I saw very few jobs, from the plant floor to the front office, that required any sex distinction. Women could fulfill the requirements of practically any job in the company. In terms of intellectual demands, there was no job that couldn't be done by any rational creature, given reasonable training, or in the case of persuasion, native ability.

Work becomes important because people have been educated to believe it is. The factory or the office is a place where one meets other people in the least threatening environment. One is provided an outlet for competition, and one can be judged, not in terms of who one is, but in terms of what one appears to be in the context of a particular group.

From this vantage point one can argue that scaling the management ladder is a questionable goal for outsiders. Blacks and women are outsiders, since they have suffered deprivation, political neglect, and even oppression. One should at least raise the question of whether they will be better off if they go into a system which is already, in my view, beginning to fail. If they do, they will probably have to begin at the bottom and work their way up. If the only way for outsiders to achieve success is through the present system of bureaucracy, we may indeed be foreclosing the future. The same energy that blacks, women, and youth are using to enter the system might better be used to transform it.

There is ample evidence that governmental and industrial managerial work can be done with fewer people. I know of three companies that are going through a recession. What have they done? They've stripped off the corporate fat from the headquarters offices. People have been fired or transferred to less attractive jobs. For years these corporations (and there are many like them) were paying people to do unnecessary work; the people are too bright not to know it. Are women sure that they want to align themselves with the corporate system, or do they want to demand different kinds of work? I think that's an important question for both blacks and women who are seeking to enter corporate and governmental bureaucracy. I suspect blacks have no choice but to get into the system, adapt to it, and try to change it from within, but women might approach the matter in another way.

It seems to me that the challenge of women might take place in an arena other than management. Women should not be led into thinking that working for GE or IBM or AT&T is the be-all and end-all. Corporate life has already exhausted its potential for providing even acceptable work for most male managerial talent. I am not opposed to women in management; I am saying that management is often hidebound and obsolete. Women may accomplish more by creating new institutions.

One approach to change could be through corporate wives. They are well aware of the demands made on executives and their families. A typical corporate wife has a poor deal. She must move her household at the whim of her husband's firm; in many cases she may not even know what her husband does. She accepts his job, even if she knows that he is not happy with it.

If she could be persuaded to be tougher, to engage in a little family consciousness-raising by asking her husband whether it's all worth it, for him and for her, she may turn out to be an explosive resource for change. She may be able to encourage her husband to be more demanding and more resistant to corporate imperatives.

135

Increasingly, for economic reasons, it's going to be possible for the many corporations to retire men early. Early retirement is a solution for firms which are overstaffed with talent. I can think of a dozen men that I know, in various companies, who are between 45 and 55 years of age, with adequate money to do what they want, who are eager to find new careers. Instead of putting more women in management, perhaps the women should be encouraging the men to get out of it.

We must find better ways to use our education to make life richer. Blacks or women can't solve this problem alone, but I am suggesting that the impetus for change in corporations and large bureaucracies may have to come from without.

In other words, corporations are not likely to make the major changes that would significantly improve the quality of work and life of those in their employ. However, there is still much that they can do to broaden the opportunities available to women whom they have treated so shabbily in the past. If they are serious about hiring women and they should be, if only because of the law, then the large corporations in this country could establish a sort of compensatory scholarship program for women who want to enter hitherto male occupations. Let them commit their scholarship funds for the next ten years to an all-out effort to attract women into engineering, law, medicine, accounting, and business.

Second, it is possible to operate offices with modular scheduling. There is no reason for everyone to spend full-time on a white-collar operation. There should be a drive to encourage management, at the cost of seeming inefficiency, to develop modular scheduling of all but the very top supervisory positions —in other words, to encourage part-time work.

In addition to modular scheduling, dispersal of work is a possible approach to the problem. Smaller programming companies are managing to stay in business because they place programming problems with women who work part-time in their own homes. With all that can be done with computers and terminals and communications, there is no reason why work cannot be decentralized and dispersed. It may even lead to the development of new social values whereby people think of work as an opportunity to have a good time.

Third, management in the white-collar world is going to have to begin to think about a tenure system. The very large organizations need to face the reality that within the management structure there already is a hidden tenure system. In order to fire a person in a large corporation one has often to document a case as if it were being taken to the Supreme Court; and the chances of losing are high. It is time we faced the fact that large firms *do* have tenure systems. Objective standards should be set, modeled perhaps on those of the American Association of University Professors (AAUP).

A system of tenure should include tenure for part-time work as well. At Sarah Lawrence, we have half-time tenure for women in teaching and administration, as well as for students. Part-time tenure for students means that if they leave they are always welcomed back, as long as they have performed satisfactorily. Employers might establish a similar policy. If an employee wishes to take off a period to do something else, to try out a different career, to engage in public service, or to have a baby, the company could promise to give that employee priority in returning. Companies would be well advised to make this a part of their personnel management policies.

If an individual has tenure, then he or she can afford to consider work in a less important, but perhaps more valuable, way. That person would value the job more because it accommodates to a total life plan.

We can never go back to the time when work was as important as it was 200 years ago. Rather we should be designing a different world in which everyone is guaranteed enough work to get by, and a chance to excell in a particular field if he chooses to work at it. There would be enough security so that anyone who decided to leave the system for a couple of years would be able to return to it. Such flexibility would carry a price, but considering what it would contribute to human satisfaction it would be a price well worth paying.

Corporations should also encourage people to invest in themselves: they should develop educational programs that are not necessarily work related. If the corporation is made up of the kind of work I think it is, then the quality of an organization is going to reflect the quality of its people, and any investment in any person has to be good for the firm. A much more liberal educational support program for employees would pay handsome returns.

Corporations might also hire more men for traditionally female jobs. In other words, prove the other side of the argument: there are no jobs that are exclusively for women.

As long as those on the outside want to get in, corporations must respond to the new political pressures by increasing the number of women entering at the bottom in all job categories. We are not going to solve the problem of thoroughly integrating the work world without bringing in people at the bottom, so that there will be a wider pool to draw upon for advancement.

Corporation appraisal systems are not as broad as they should be. They should be both broader and more standard, so that women, men, blacks, whites, old, young, can be measured against a standard criterion that would show who has potential. Grafted onto that should be measurement against a range of jobs as opposed to having personnel measure up only to a particular job description with appraisal zeroed to that.

It is also going to be necessary to create more leisure time and more disposable time, particularly at the bottom of the economic ladder. The more disposable time people have, the more they are going to learn. Perhaps a guaranteed annual income would be a good place to begin. With more disposable time and income at the command of the public, our educational system should focus more on the arts: the performing arts, creative arts, liberal arts. This may sound idealistic but I believe that there are commercial opportunities to be exploited in meeting leisure needs. We need an educational commitment that is antipragmatic that has nothing to do with earning but lots to do with spending.

The changes that are taking place in our society have to do with rights: civil rights, property rights, and the new right to a lifestyle—the right to lead a personal life determined by one's own values. Everyone except perhaps those at the very top of the establishment, is involved in a battle for these rights: women, blacks, other minorities, and youth.

What concerns me is that demands for rights are generally expressed negatively, in terms of protection from something or as minimal guarantees. They are estimates of security formulated in terms of minimum risk. It is tragic that a society with such incredible potential still conceptualizes the new life of the future in negative terms. We should fight instead to expand and utilize our potential.

It is amazing that at this point in history, television reflects so little of the social change going on in this country. It does not even begin to reflect the reality of women's lives. Scholars and politicians should encourage change here, so that instead of relying on the East Coast and a few metropolitan centers, the whole country realizes that there is not just a woman's problem, or a black problem, but a national problem. In this respect, business could undertake to support programs of better communication on the condition of women.

Lastly, we need more programs of supportive education. My predecessor at Sarah Lawrence instituted a Center for Continuing Education, which serves women whose children are at least reasonably on their own. It prepares these women for a variety of careers and has been successful in that task. More than that, however, the center has increased the self-awareness of these women. Through corporations and government, similar ways should be developed for all people in their early middle years—I happen to think that this is especially urgent for men—to be able to shift from one occupation to another.

People need to be able to get out of their ruts, to use their education and experience in creative ways, and to have the chance to reexamine their lives and contribute meaningfully to society. That is, after all, the point of liberation.

13
Challenge and Resolution

Eli Ginzberg

This concluding chapter has a twofold objective. It summarizes briefly the principal findings and recommendations contained in the preceding presentations and it provides me with an opportunity to elaborate on selected themes.

The conference on which this volume is based focused on four dimensions of women's challenge to management: analysis, directions for action, problematics, and historical perspective. All of the participants accept the basic thesis that increasing numbers of women are indeed demanding equal consideration in competing for the better jobs in the economy. However the implications of the challenge were approached from different vantage points, generally emphasizing either the view of the challengers (women who seek high level employment) or that of the challenged (employers of managerial personnel). In the former, the analysis centered primarily upon the forces that have shaped women's life styles and that have led to increasing female dissatisfaction with the status quo. The latter approach examined the managerial function and explored employer attitudes and behavior toward upgrading the female labor force. These approaches are of course complementary, and it was recognized that underlying women's actions and employers' reactions is the value system of the larger society.

Thus, considerable attention was paid to exploring the cultural and economic factors that have produced differential expectations for the sexes. It was accepted that an interplay of social forces had served to give ascendancy to the female role of full-time homemaker, with its dual effect of lowering feminine work expectations and of deterring employers from considering women as serious competitors for high status employment.

Attitudes are shaped early in life, and when girls learn that primacy is given to male work goals, they plan their courses of action accordingly. Since all discriminatory systems have a built-in dynamic that leads those who are discriminated against to supply a rationale for bias, female conformance to societal norms has served as justification for differential treatment of the sexes. Because its roots go deep into every facet of our society, with women as well as men acting to reinforce existing preconceptions about proper female roles, sex discrimination is exceptionally difficult to eliminate. However, despite prior conditioning and the continuing pervasiveness of the "feminine mystique," it was recognized that significant changes are occurring that will slowly but surely result in continuing modifications in women's traditional role.

The question of family size is a key determinant of the career opportunities available to women. We appear to be in a period when small families will increasingly be the norm as a result of personal preference, the availability of improved birth control techniques, and widening legalization of abortion. Hence, fewer and fewer women will leave the labor force or, if they do, it will be for a shorter time. Women workers in the future will represent a less distinctive and differentiated labor supply than in the past.

The greatest danger in dealing with a rapidly changing situation involving minorities—and in this context we view women as a minority—is to project past experience. In a rapidly changing situation, such projections are certain to be wrong. To continue to postulate a high female withdrawal rate from the labor force will probably turn out to be an erroneous projection.

A related point refers to the future educational achievements of women. The dip in the curve of women with higher degrees has been reversed: more women are in medical school; more are in law school; and female recipients of Ph.D.s are increasing, although the ratio is still below the peak of the 1920s. The rationalization that women hold poor jobs because of their failure to invest in higher education is becoming untenable. The more education they acquire, the more formidable competitors they will be for the limited number of good job openings that are available.

However, there is some question about the number of women who are oriented to management. There is no real tradition of women in leadership roles in the business world. Even in female occupations, executive positions are held largely by males. Thus, while there is little doubt that many women qualify for managerial employment, it is an open question whether large numbers will move toward managerial careers without special encouragement and support.

Some women are undoubtedly moving under their own momentum, much more so than in the past. Our society is an amalgam of special interest groups. Everybody fights with everybody else for a bigger piece of the action. Historically, women have not been sufficiently organized to wage successful battles. Now they have begun to organize themselves far more efficiently than in the past, and one must postulate an increase in the effectiveness of their challenge. It is hard to believe that their cooperative effort will break up and that they will disappear as a pressure group. The probabilities are high that their joint actions will intensify.

The general egalitarian thrust, heavily influenced by the racial revolution and reinforced by the youth revolution, can have only positive effects upon the women's revolution. We live in a society where strong forces for change are at work, and the women's movement is part of these larger social adjustments.

It was generally acknowledged that pervasive discrimination against women in large organizations—private, nonprofit, and public—has existed, presently exists, and will probably continue to exist for a long time. No one asserted that what happens to women in the marketplace reflects competitive realities rather than employer discrimination. No one claimed that women get "what they deserve" because they lack requisite education, skill, or motivation. While role differentiation can account for the relative scarcity of female aspirants for high level positions, considerable evidence was adduced that women with proper credentials have been unable to move into preferred employment in business, government, or universities to the same extent as men.

There is no question that personnel policies affecting women are influenced by social attitudes, but there appears to be a significant time lag between changes in the status of women and management's recognition of female interest in and competence to perform leadership functions. It was pointed out that the executive wife has been touted as a full-time helpmate, and this may deflect many executives from appointing women to other than subsidiary positions. However, the crux of the matter is whether most employers who believe that they have been doing very well without female managerial personnel can be persuaded to change their habits and accept what to most of them is an unknown, untried, and upsetting innovation.

Few doubted that an assault upon male-dominated strongholds would meet with a great deal of resistance, but all recognized the increasing strength of the female assailants and agreed that they would eventually prevail. Moreover, no one questioned that a successful challenge to management would result in widespread changes affecting all employees in the employing organizations. One cannot make significant changes in a manpower system without influencing and transforming its many subcomponents. For example, in the comparable movement to open up more opportunities for blacks, selection procedures, recruitment policies, personnel support systems, marketing tactics, and community strategies have undergone considerable reevaluation and revision. The same turbulence is likely to ensue as progress is made in improving the position of women.

Furthermore, a positive response to women's challenge to management will result in societal repercussions since alterations in traditional employment relationships will certainly have large scale reverberations beyond the labor market.

In exploring directions for action, it was emphasized that those who have the most to gain must assume the primary responsibility. Women must become more knowledgeable and more sophisticated in manipulating the various systems for their own benefit. One cannot realize opportunities for other people. One can help them, support them, show them the way, encourage them, even train them, but finally, the responsibility for change rests with the party of primary interest. And that is a difficult task, since women have been on the periphery for so long.

One striking difference between racial and ethnic minorities and women is that women, particularly white middle class women, have more opportunity to learn how the system operates through their fathers and husbands. Poor blacks and other outsiders don't have anybody high in the system to whom they can turn for help. But many white women have knowledgeable male relatives and friends who can supply them with critically useful information. Informal communications networks serve as important informational and hiring channels. Many women who seek managerial level jobs have access to such a network. Women who are reluctant to utilize personal contacts need to be reminded that men have always made use of such contacts.

It is well to remember that the men who are prejudiced against women and discriminate against them are the sons of women. Therefore women face the challenge of doing a better job of raising their sons, not only as potential employers of women, but as future husbands who will encourage and support their wives' work aspirations. Moreover, mothers carry much responsibility for the low career aspirations of their daughters. Thus, they have a wide area for constructive action. Since women are the major nurturing agents in our society, they must take the lead in breaking down sex stereotypes. It is true that they operate in a society pervaded with sex prejudice and discrimination, of which they themselves are victims. However, as the society begins to lower discriminatory barriers, mothers must be prepared to encourage their children to respond positively to the new forces.

Women must also make greater efforts to get into positions of influence in organizations that have a high potential for accelerating change. While women have been voting for more than 50 years, they have a very poor record as elected and appointed public officials. They haven't pressed hard enough for their share of the limited, and therefore highly valued, political plums. Since political action can be a great force for social change, women must organize and fight for larger representation in government if they wish to speed their progress.

Women are members of trade unions and yet they have made limited progress as members of the union hierarchy. They comprise the majority of workers in large governmental bureaucracies such as school systems; yet they have seldom if ever challenged the sex discrimination that has systematically prevented them from moving into the highest positions. Women have much to do to reshape the organizations of which they are a part, so that these institutions will be more responsive to their needs.

In these several efforts it is desirable that they seek and find allies with whom they can form coalitions. There are some men in positions of power who now appear to be willing to cooperate with women in breaking down sex barriers. The male peers of women students in professional and graduate schools can also be useful. Often people in a position to help will do so, but only if they are prodded. The prodding technique has much to commend it. Women probably have many potential allies who will not activate themselves but will respond if asked to help.

However, reminders and prodding will not be sufficient to move many men from their rigidly fixed positions. Then stronger actions such as sit-ins, picketing, boycotts, and other harassment techniques may be in order. Women who are serious about moving aggressively against discrimination must be willing on occasion to adopt unladylike tactics.

One must not minimize the hard work that women must do to

collect money, build staffs, and construct their own organizations. Here is one place where black efforts can serve as models. Our racial problem would be much further from solution were it not for the National Association for the Advancement of Colored People, the Urban League, the Southern Christian Leadership Conference, and similar groups. They took the lead to create an environment predisposed for change and they did the hard work of fighting cases through the courts. To the extent that more and more women become interested in their own progress, they must do much better than rely on the American Association of University Women or the Business and Professional Women's Clubs, useful as these organizations have been. This means much more organization, staff, money, and programs.

Now what about management's actions? The analysis suggested that management will move faster or slower, depending upon the amount of pressure to which it is subjected. Management has the primary task of keeping an organization going—to treat patients, educate students, make a profit—depending on its mission or goal. It will respond to new demands only to the extent that it is forced to deal with them. Good management tries to stay one step ahead of the changing environment. If it sees things happening on the equal opportunity front, it will try to get more women into middle and top management. It will recognize that it must make an effort. No smart management wants to be a straggler in the parade.

Moreover, management is highly imitative. If one large organization discovers that another is doing something new, it will probably follow suit and soon most managements will fall in line. Managers like company; they crowd into the same boat. No management likes to get too far out ahead or lag too far behind.

In seeking women for higher level positions, management should, in the first instance, look at its own pool of female talent which is often considerable. Of course, it may hesitate to do so, fearing that if it finds many talented women in the pool, it will brand itself as having been incompetent. It is not easy for employers to acknowledge that women whom it refused repeatedly to consider for promotion are suddenly promotable.

But management may find it better to swallow that pill because the best device for selecting people for promotion, perhaps the only reliable one, is the quality of their performance in the specific work environment. If sex is no longer a barrier, then women within the organization deserve to be looked at with care, since there is likely to be a much larger supply of latent talent than most people surmise.

Employers must also improve their external recruitment. First they will have to decide on the criteria to use in selecting women, in order to assure equality of opportunity. They also must locate pools of candidates who are oriented to management. Women with baccalaureate degrees, business school graduates, as well as certain professional students such as lawyers, should be sought for such positions. It may even be in the employer's interest to subsidize the education of young women interested in entering male fields. In any event, university placement offices can prove to be a major referral source but only if management is serious about changing its spots, convinces the placement staff that it is reforming, and proves by its hiring and promotion policies that it is in fact no longer discriminating against women. College and university staffs are too sophisticated to play along with the employer who talks well but whose actions belie his words.

Management faces a difficult task in breaking down conventional male-female job classifications. Every job should be open to members of either sex. That doesn't mean that most production managers in the future will be women, but it does mean that an occasional production manager may be a woman.

It was recognized that considerable corporate education must be undertaken if the new policy toward women is to be effective. It is not enough that the president of the company is interested in promoting women. He is interested in a thousand issues—that is, if he is an effective top executive. And increasing opportunities for women are not likely to be near the top of his agenda. For example, given the complex problems that a cabinet officer faces, he cannot be expected to spend more than a half hour twice a year on expanding opportunities for women under his jurisdiction. The most one can ask of him is to delegate this task

147

to a senior administrator and to direct him to push his policy and to persuade middle management, which is often indifferent or hostile, that he means what he says.

Antinepotism rules can safely be discarded, even while protecting the integrity of the organization. One way in which a conflict of interest can be avoided is to see that neither spouse is directly responsible for evaluating the work of the other.

A strong plea was made for facilitating leaves of absence for women without loss of benefits. Some women will want or need to take considerable time off to raise their children, but many will return within a short time, and they should be encouraged to do so if they wish.

Another issue relates to the actions that corporations can take to facilitate the relocation of female managers. They should seek to work out cooperative relations with other firms that face the same problem of finding a job for one family member when they want to relocate a spouse. Increasingly, organizations that must reassign a male executive will have to find a position for his working wife. We have seen the beginnings of this trend to family placement in the armed forces and in the State Department. And a few corporations and universities are exploring how they can act to ease this problem.

Corporations have long cooperated with each other in placing the sons of senior executives. Now they will be asked to do the same for wives. In general, it is not considered cricket to bring your son into your own organization. It creates too many problems. But it is customary to ask the head of another corporation to take your boy in and to do the same for him.

With respect to governmental actions, it was acknowledged that the Department of Labor's Revised Order Number 4 is probably the most significant single development in speeding the employment of women at high occupational levels. Increasing public concern with this problem bespeaks a growing awareness of the potential impact of this regulation. The pressures that women have exerted to achieve equal employment opportunity have borne fruit in various legislative and administrative developments which foreshadow the ratification of the equal rights amendment.

For the near future, the actions of the Office of Federal Contract Compliance will exercise the principal leverage by pressing the country's largest employers to produce affirmative action plans and to live up to them.

The manner of implementation of Order Number 4 remains to be revealed: no one can be sure how much pressure the government will exert; the goals that it will accept as reasonable; the time that it will allow for the goals to be reached. Government will probably move cautiously in response to conflicting political pressures. As it gains experience in enforcing the order, it will probably get tougher, because when it finds that one company can meet requirements, the next firm will not be able to plead hardship. It will be years before the situation will be clarified, but it is certain that the employment picture will never again be the same. The pressure is on and it can go in only one direction—up!

Another arena of public action relates to day care facilities for children of working mothers. The relevance of public child care facilities for managerial and executive personnel is unclear, since these mothers' incomes are likely to permit them to make private arrangements for their offspring. However, a small number of corporations and nonprofit institutions may find it relatively easy to operate facilities on their premises for their employees' children. If employers had no alternative but to establish child care facilities to attract and retain their female work force, they would do so. While employees do not usually attain managerial rank when they are young, women who aim for high level posts may require day care assistance during their early period of employment. For these women, publicly financed centers can make the difference between a continuing employment relationship leading to better jobs or involuntary withdrawal from the labor force.

The educational system is an important mechanism for effecting changes in female attitudes and expectations. Schools have tended to reinforce differential family expectations for boys and girls. From their earliest years, girls are encouraged to engage in "feminine" pursuits and discouraged from enrolling in "male" courses. Guidance counselors have been notorious purveyors of

149

sex-typed information which presents restricted options to girls. Pressures for change in occupational patterning cannot be effectuated unless young girls early become aware of their many available options and are encouraged to pursue their choice.

Now let us look at the problematics. I want to share certain uncertainties about issues which remain to be resolved.

First we must remember that the number of good jobs in every organization is distinctly limited, that the competition for these jobs is severe, and that most white males lose out. There are many disgruntled males in business, disgruntled because they didn't make it.

Many people do not enjoy working for a large organization. It becomes that much less exciting once they recognize that they are not going anywhere. So we have to remember that business is highly competitive and that there is not much room at the top. With the many competing for the few good jobs it is not easy to work out reasonable targets for women in higher management. That's an assignment that must still be met.

What does good progress mean in terms of increasing the number and proportion of women in the middle and higher echelons? What are realistic goals? The answers are complicated by the fact that many veterans and many black male college graduates are active competitors for the same few good jobs.

Black women must also be filtered into this complex, competitive situation. In my view it would be wrong for them to withdraw from the competition in order to make it easier for black men to move up the executive ladder. I believe that this would be a bad strategy, because no one who withdraws from the race can assure who the winner will be. No group controls the job market. I think everybody who is interested in competing must compete. We must move as quickly as possible toward a society which is color-blind, sex-blind, age-blind—in short a society that has eliminated discrimination.

There are situations where community groups have gained control over a block of jobs. If the blacks in New York or Detroit secure control over hospitals, school boards, and welfare centers, they may decide on a policy that gives preference to men.

However, I question whether and for how long such a policy is likely to be effective.

We talked of youths as allies of women. This is true from one point of view, but not from another. If the employment situation remains unsatisfactory, I don't think that many young men will go out of their way to help women. It is easier to be helpful in a world in which there is lots of opportunity. We face an awkward situation regarding the outlook for educated manpower in the near future. The supply and demand relationships, especially for those holding the doctorate, are seriously awry. If the outlook is ominous for males, it is difficult to be optimistic about the prospects for women.

The next issue is also confused: One can postulate an anti-materialistic bias on the part of many upper income, well-educated youth which is associated with a negativism on their part toward devoting all their energies to maximizing their income. They do not want to kill themselves for their employers. To the extent that this is true of males from upper income homes one must ask whether it also reflects the attitudes of girls from this same strategic group. If so, we had better not jump too quickly to conclusions about their career drives.

We had stray references to technology. Technology can cut several ways. It was predicted that women will be able to work at home with the aid of new communications devices. Technology may also facilitate flexibility in work scheduling. On the other hand, technology threatens to eliminate many clerical and middle management jobs, from which many women might otherwise gain access to higher level jobs.

A study of womanpower was placed on the agenda of the National Manpower Council fifteen years ago by a single vote since the minority did not consider it worthwhile to probe the subject in depth. There are two ways of looking at the last fifteen years. One is to bemoan the slow progress that has been made to reduce and eliminate discrimination against women. The other is to recognize the big leap forward between the council's study of womanpower and Order Number 4.

We should not minimize the support that the sex revolution

has received from the racial revolution. It is inevitable that, as the American people begin to eliminate the pathology long present in white-black relations, this sanitizing will have a carry-over effect on male-female relations.

The congruence of the black and female revolutions will be mutually supportive, even though they may find themselves from time to time in competition with each other. But, for the long pull, the women's revolution will be accelerated by the institutional changes precipitated by black progress.

Powerful constraints pervade the family, school, church, philanthropy, the university, business organizations, government; and nobody should assume that these complex institutions can be turned around overnight. On the other hand, if one is acquainted with recent developments in the Catholic Church and the U.S. Army—two most tradition-bound institutions—one is forced to conclude that liberalization can take place. Who would have believed that a cardinal would publicly criticize the Pope or that a general on active duty would testify that in his opinion almost every army policy, program, and procedure now in place must be altered if the army is to deal effectively with its new recruits? These illustrations suggest that we are in effect living in a revolutionary period.

Clearly, women are reaching new levels of consciousness, and this is critical, for unless people who are discriminated against are aware of it, they will be unable to do anything to change matters. Their consciousness of being discriminated against has reached a point that can only lead to further change. This will largely be a function of the pressure that women exert and the degree of resistance that they will meet. We may be overestimating both forces. Women may not push as hard as some anticipate, but neither may the critical institutions be as resistant as others predict.

One point in conclusion. We have addressed ourselves to the problems of women as a group and in the process have also discussed the problems of racial and ethnic minorities. But while we must think and act in terms of groups, we must never lose sight of the fact that the real challenge that our democratic society faces is to broaden opportunity for each individual.

Selected Bibliography

Cain, Glen. *Married Women in the Labor Force*. Chicago: University of Chicago Press, 1966.

Epstein, Cynthia Fuchs. *Woman's Place: Options and Limits in Professional Careers*. Berkeley: University of California Press, 1970.

Fogarty, Michael P.; Allen, A. J.; Allen, Isobel; and Walters, Patricia. *Women in Top Jobs*. London: Allen and Unwin, 1971.

Fogarty, Michael P., with Rhona and Robin Rapoport. *Women in Top Jobs: The Next Step*. PEP Research Report, vol. 28, Broadsheet 535. London: PEP, March 1972.

Ginzberg, Eli, and Associates. *Life Styles of Educated Women*. New York: Columbia University Press, 1966.

Ginzberg, Eli, and Yohalem, Alice M. *Educated American Women: Self-Portraits*. New York: Columbia University Press, 1966.

Janeway, Elizabeth. *Man's World and Woman's Place*. New York: Morrow, 1971.

Kreps, Juanita. *Sex in the Marketplace: American Women at Work*. Baltimore: The John Hopkins Press, 1971.

National Manpower Council. *Womanpower*. New York: Columbia University Press, 1957.

Oppenheimer, Valerie Kincade. *The Female Labor Force in the United States: Demographic and Economic Factors Governing its Growth and Changing Composition*. Berkeley: Institute of International Studies, University of California, 1970.

Smuts, Robert W. *Women and Work in America*. New York: Columbia University Press, 1959.